ART IN AMERICA

ART IN AMERICA

From Colonial Days
Through the Nineteenth Century

ROBERT MYRON / ABNER SUNDELL

CROWELL-COLLIER PRESS
Collier-Macmillan Limited, London

5067

CONTENTS

"What is most distinctive about America?" the traveler is often asked. "When you look about this country what differentiates it most from Europe?"

The answer is quite often the same. "The white wooden houses standing alone in the country, which gather closer to become suburbs, and then, grouped around a white church, each set back on its own lawn, become a town. In European towns the houses are drab gray or beige stone, attached on either side to other houses, surrounded by high walls, or built directly onto the sidewalk. But when I think of America I think of the houses—the white wooden houses on the bright green lawns."

It is not strange that the house creates the strongest impression of America. Because it was the house that was America's first art form; the carpenter the first creator of an American visual image. It was toward shelter that all actions were directed in mighty and sustained effort as the New World was settled, and it was toward the improvement

[I]

THE
PRACTICAL
PURITAN

and decoration of this shelter that the arts of America began their growth. Not for gods or tombs or kings, not for cathedrals or courts or temples, were the art traditions of America shaped, but for the practicable, serviceable function of the individual citizen. Just as the land and society were shaped, not for ruler, but for subject, so the visual arts—architecture, painting, sculpture—were shaped, not for the palace but for the home.

The house did not become the distinctive American work of art by forethought. Indeed, quite the opposite was intended. No sooner had the first settlers emerged from the huts, hovels, wigwams, and tents that had been their protection during their first harsh winters, than they began to construct permanent habitation. Their first attempts were to bring to the New World what they had had in the old, to perpetuate the cultural forms with which they were familiar. The pockets of culture they hewed out of the wilderness were capsule-sized imitations of the European towns and cities from which they had come. The first settlers were not architects. They were colonists, fortunate if carpenters were numbered among their party. They built from memory, modifying and transforming by frontier necessity, using their ingenuity to improvise and vary the traditional themes according to materials available, building in a hurry to provide shelter for the unsheltered and protection from the natives.

The American tradition of improvisation—in building, in art, in our entire society—the philosophy of "the difficult we do immediately, the impossible takes a little longer," which is so much a part of our culture, started as the settler, ax in hand, faced the timbers of the wilderness and transformed them into the beams of his home. The stone, brick, and clay building materials indigenous to the mountains and soil of western Europe were replaced by the wood of eastern America's forested shores. The ax, the adz, the saw, the hammer, and the plane replaced the more sophisticated technological tools of stonecutting, masonry, and clay-firing, which had all been left behind. And small, mostly wooden duplicates of English, Dutch, French, Spanish, and Scandinavian villages came into being around the harbors of the New World.

Verrazano, Cartier, de Soto, Coronado, Raleigh, Hudson—whose names were given to the first American forts and rivers—were international adventurers who bridged the oceans, dropped anchor in the harbors, took the islands and held them against savage nature and often savage natives, in the names of the kings and commercial monopolies of Europe.

The Spaniards were the first on the North American continent. Moving north from conquests in Mexico where Cortez had destroyed the Aztec and Mayan Indian civilizations, the conquistadores crossed the Rio Grande. Between the sixteenth and eighteenth centuries they established a string of military forts and Catholic missions in the southern part of what is now the United States—in Texas, Arizona, New Mexico, southern California, and Florida. Their policy was to extract work and wealth through force and taxes, to admit only Catholic settlers, and to Christianize the Indians—in other words, to transplant feudalism to the wilderness. Just as their ancestors of the fifteenth century had incorporated Moorish traditions in their buildings in Spain, the Spanish colonists absorbed the architectural patterns of the Southwest Indians and adapted the design of the Pueblos as they built their homes in the New World.

In the north, the French moved down from Champlain's stronghold in Quebec—into the Mohawk Valley, westward along the Wisconsin River, and south along the Mississippi. As the Indian tribes were converted to Catholicism, French forts were built from Montreal to Mobile. In these wooden communities protected by palisade walls, imported trifles of furniture, clothes, music, and dance gave the settlers a small echo of the brilliant cultural life they had left behind in Paris. Fur traders brought news as they traveled up and down the rivers in flat-bottomed wooden boats carrying the precious furs from the frozen wastes of Canada to the ports of New Orleans, Biloxi, and Mobile.

Henry Hudson claimed New Netherlands for the Dutch in 1609. The Dutch West Indies Company changed New Amsterdam from a small walled fort to a small town, and the Hudson River was host to hundreds of enterprising Dutch farmers and trappers. Walled forts were built that are now the cities of Kingston and Albany. From New Amsterdam the Dutch sailed from Cape Cod to Delaware Bay and up the Connecticut River, and the sails of their high-pooped, broad-bottomed ships were seen by the patroons in their lordly stone houses and by tenants and villagers in the hamlets that were miniatures of their Old World originals.

For fifty-five years the Dutch ruled, until New Amsterdam was ceded to the English and New Amsterdam became New York. When that happened there were six other British colonies on the Atlantic coast—at Plymouth and Boston in Massachusetts, Jamestown in Virginia, and New Hampshire, Connecticut, and Rhode Island. Before the end of the seventeenth century, twelve thriving British colonies were strung along the eastern tidewater.

England's claim to the New World was built on the discovery of the continent by Cabot in 1497, and it was solidified by the defeat of the Spanish Armada in 1588. England was ruled by the court, the Anglican church, and a mighty landed aristocracy, backed up and supported by a vast and powerful fleet. Joint stock companies were formed—cooperative ventures financed by business, manned by the public, and protected by the court. They sought new materials—fish, furs, agricultural products, and lumber—and prepared England for the outward flow of colonists.

Economic panics in England, crop failures, rising food prices, and unemployment sent the mass movement on its way. Between 1620 and 1635, 70,000 English migrated to America and the West Indies.

It was the English, more than the Spanish, French, or Dutch, who shaped America, the language, art, and social structure we have today. It was the English who molded the New World's culture.

Specifically, the story of American art began as the Puritans set foot on Plymouth Rock in 1620. Although they were only a handful of settlers, the history and character of America was born with their arrival. Led and dominated by powerful religious leaders, they were here to build a city of God, a city on a hill, firm in the belief that the eyes of the world would be riveted on what they were creating.

Dedicated Protestants—Calvinists—who were driven out of Europe because of their dissent with the Catholic and Anglican churches, they formed the unyielding background of American colonialism. Their insistence on hard work, their shrewdness, ingenuity, patience, temperance, sobriety, thrift, ambition, and stubborn individualism were the basic qualities necessary for survival.

Craftsmen, farmers, small businessmen—together with the poor, the dispossessed, the landless, the hungry, the servants of others anxious to work out their servitude—these were the people who built America, whose militant faith had the force and energy to civilize the land and eventually to assimilate and transform all other colonists. Their attitudes and values became the attitudes and values of America.

Land was abundant. Labor was in short supply. Rewards were great for artisans. Small merchants could become industrialists, tenant farmers could be landowners. Puritanism appealed to merchants because it taught that man could serve God as well as his business or profession, and that all callings were equally honorable. "Work hard to please God," they taught. "In serving man one serves God."

Between 1628 and 1630, fifteen boats brought 1,000 pilgrims. Four years later 10,000 Puritans were in New England. The most immediate problems after the landing on Plymouth Rock were refuge, security, livelihood, and defense. And until these demands could be met, there was no time for the arts. If a toehold were to be established in this cold and hostile wilderness, practical problems had to come first.

People dug themselves into caves and pits in the hillsides and riverbanks and hammered together lean-tos and makeshift tents, huts and hovels, from ships' canvas, casks, and shipping crates. Some even lived in simple shelters resembling the wigwams of the Indians, made of bent-over saplings covered with sod and thatch. Then with amazing speed, ingenuity, and improvisation, with the tools and materials on hand, they built wood frame houses as similar as possible under the circumstances to the remembered image of homes they had left behind in England.

Trees were cut and logs became planks and timbers, mortar was made from lime, and window areas were filled with oiled cloth and paper. Logs were hewn into square and rectangular beams, and in the same way many houses are built today, the wall frames were joined on the ground and raised into position on the foundations. They were fixed in place with wooden pins and steep roof timbers were set atop them. Spaces between the wall beams were filled with wattle and daub, brick or plaster, and sheathed on the outside with clapboards, shingles, or planks. The inside walls were planked up and the roofs were reinforced with cross timbers and covered with thatch and rushes. There were at most one or two rooms, with a loft upstairs beneath the high pitched roof. Within a few years bricks were being made to reinforce the foundations and glass was placed in the window frames.

Professional architects were nonexistent. The builders were self-taught carpenters who learned by trial and error and were guided more by the pressures of time, available materials, and the amount of cooperation they could get from their fellow settlers than by building plans or other factors. Houses were built of planks, shingles, and timbers and held in place with wooden pegs, hand-wrought nails, luck, and the ambition, intuition, and industry of the builders. Simple Cape Cod houses built today look much like the Puritan houses that sprang up those first few years along Massachusetts' savage shore.

Log cabins which are the popular image of early colonial homes were not introduced by the English but by the Swedish and Finnish settlers of Delaware who had lived in log cabins for centuries in their native Scandinavia.

Because stone had to be quarried some distance from the first villages, it was not commonly used, except for foundations and cooking hearths. It was not until 1679, when a great fire almost wiped out Boston, that stone and brick became the common material for chimneys.

The great artistic achievement of the Puritans was improvisation—the art of making beauty from materials readily at hand. Puritan art was practical and functional. Use was the essence. The homes, like the people who inhabited them, were plain, stark, and austere. Brown was the color of their wood as God had made it, and brown was overwhelmingly the color of their homes, inside and out. English homes were the model, but each man shaped his own to his individual needs. Just as the Puritan broke away from the Church of England and shaped his religion to his own needs, so was his home a breakaway from English construction, shaped to his own individual use, need, and purpose.

Directness was a dominant characteristic of the Puritan, and it shows indelibly in his use of materials. Beams functioned not only as support and reinforcement, but as decoration. They were neither hidden nor covered but displayed in all the richness and natural beauty of hand-hewn wood. Lines of structure and separation were dominant visually. And later, when purposeful decoration began, line became the essence of Puritan art.

Though the outside of these early American homes remained simple, the interiors showed a growing concern with decoration. This can be seen in the wood carving on furniture, the hammered designs on copper cooking utensils and silver tableware.

The Puritan was a doer, not a thinker. Meditation was not part of his philosophy since it might lead to abstract thought, a dangerous pastime that sometimes led to questioning of authority, a practice which was very close to heresy. Therefore the kind of art that required meditation was suspect. Calvin had warned, "Men should not paint or carve anything but such as can be seen with the eye; so that God's majesty which is too exalted for human sight may not be corrupted by fantasies which have no true agreement therewith."

The Puritan could enjoy moderate finery in his dress and furnishings, just so long as the man of small means did not take on the airs or trappings of the gentleman. And he built, painted, and carved with the same spirit. His place of worship was a meetinghouse for the congregation's use, not a museum to house stone saints. The Puritan hated the word church and would not build one in America. He permitted neither the cross nor the spire. He rejected stained glass windows because the colors got in the way of God's pure sunlight, and images of saints, organ music, chants, and choirs because they threw a jeweled curtain between man and God. His meetinghouse was crowned with a central tower which held the bell and supported a practical weather vane. His architect was a carpenter, his sculptor the man who made the weather vane or carved the death head on gravestones or enriched the beams of his house through hand-hewing. Painters made shop signs and coffin decorations and showed men as they looked and moved. They did not portray fables which the human eye had never seen, nor paint biblical episodes which suggested private knowledge of God beyond the holy words inscribed in the Bible.

During the latter part of the seventeenth century and in the beginning of the eighteenth, the use of stone became more common. Houses grew higher and wider, thatch was replaced on roofs by more durable tiles, slates, and shingles, windows were reinforced with wooden or iron casements, and wooden chimneys were almost all replaced with either stone or brick. Buildings were elaborated upon, ornamented and refined and a man's house could show his proud English heritage and his financial position in the community.

Now, with the pressures of time and shelter removed, new buildings were constructed from builder's guides that had been brought over from the old country. But almost always variations were made in traditional plans as homes were adjusted to individual tastes and needs and materials. As more room was needed a homeowner might continue his roof downward and fill in the space below the overhang with additional rooms. In this way the saltbox house, so called because of its shape, was created.

Homes in English villages had been built with two stories, the second jutting beyond the lower to form an overhang under which a merchant and his wares could be protected from the weather, so the colonists began to build two-story houses in the New World, with the overhang designed in such a way that muskets could fit through small openings to allow the residents to defend themselves against attack. A liveliness, reminiscent of

Elizabethan England was added through the use of decorated brackets under the jutting second story, carved pendants or drops at the corners, ornaments on the house peaks or gables, and chimneys which no longer were simple four-sided exterior shapes but clustered forms in the center as the expanding house surrounded it. Inside, the staircases had pendants too, and bulbous balusters and ornaments of finely turned and carved wood.

The Reverend Joseph Capen had a prosperous father-in-law who saw to it that his daughter and her esteemed husband lived in a fine home that befitted his position. The Capen House, built in 1683 in Topsfield, Massachusetts, is typical of the finest homes built in the Puritan colonies toward the end of the seventeenth century. The huge kitchen fireplace, built both for cooking and warmth, spanned half the length of the room, with a huge oak beam, sixteen inches square, serving as the lintel. The molded edges of the horizontal and vertical sheathing in the two downstairs rooms suggested the Reverend's status, and the exposed

The Capen House, built in 1683 in Topsfield, Massachusetts. COURTESY OF THE CAPEN HOUSE

ceiling beams and wall planks, the wide plank flooring and the solid basic wooden furniture gave the house a warm, intimate, and protective feeling.

Many modern houses built in America today are remarkably like this Puritan home. Even as architects did in the Renaissance in Europe, modern American architects have been seeking the beauty of function. They have been able to accomplish this through a revival of the earliest American building forms, with their prominent fireplaces, functional structure, and exposed beams—and through elaborate use of the classical American building material, wood.

The late Frank Lloyd Wright, one of the greatest of American architects, championed this American Renaissance, giving testimony to the fact that our colonial heritage is not buried in history but is a vital and living stimulation, inspiring contemporary artists and affecting present-day homes, furnishings, and decorations.

The interior of the Capen House had the charm of many variations of the color brown—soft, textured wood grains of the forest, warm reds of the fireplace bricks, soft whites of plastered walls, and the handsomely-shaped carved and decorated chests, bedsteads, tables, and chairs. Much of the furniture was built and decorated according to traditional English Gothic forms, but furnishings, like the houses, were given individual motifs to suit the personality of the owner.

The Puritan town was square and compact, with houses huddled closely about the meetinghouse, which was town hall, church, schoolhouse, and business center all rolled into one. There was no European tradition for the meetinghouse. It was strictly a New England Puritan innovation, undoubtedly caused by the fact that the Puritans, always a European minority, were suddenly an American majority, in control of their church, schools, and government. Great, gaunt clapboard buildings, standing two to three stories high, the meetinghouses were as plain, forthright, and severe as the Puritan preachers. But only on the outside. The inside was warm with polished woods, and decorations reflected the Puritan's happiness and hope in God and the buoyant humility of his faith. Simple, sturdy, strong as the mighty oaks that provided its timbers, with its public face quiet and its private face exuberant and joyous, the meetinghouse exemplified the American character of the late seventeenth century. The characteristics of the Puritan meetinghouse still exemplify much of America today.

The same colors, the browns, ochers, reds, and whites that were the colors of their homes, were the colors the Puritans used in their paintings when they found time to paint. There had been no architects in the beginning, just men willing to try their hands at building, nor were there professional artists. The same practical carpenters, sign painters, and merchants became the self-taught painters, producing the practical portraits demanded by those who could afford such luxuries. Portraits of owner and family contributed individuality to a house, they told who lived there and what he looked like and gave a home the stamp of a family's presence. Landscapes, historical, and still life scenes were frivolous and impractical, and religious painting appealed to the emotions and went beyond the simple practicality of their religion. Therefore, when Puritans did start to paint, they produced workable, practical portraits for their middle-class patrons. Unlike Europe or Asia, where art was produced for emperors, kings, popes, courts, tombs, temples, and churches, American art was produced for a prosperous middle class, by untrained artists of that same middle class.

The first Puritan portraits were painted to the best of the amateur painter's ability in a style based on that of the most popular court painters of the era. Hans Holbein had been court painter to Henry VIII during the previous century. Copies and engravings of his work had circulated throughout England and Holland, and many lesser known English and European painters had imitated him. Thus, by the seventeenth century when the Puritans sailed for America, they were familiar with Holbein's style, and some of the pilgrim fathers brought pictures and engravings with them to give their homes in the New World a touch of the comforts and culture they had left behind.

It was only natural, therefore, that the first paintings executed in the colonies were very much in the idiom of Holbein, with hard and precise outlines, emphasis on contour and little modeling of facial features. Features were drawn onto the faces almost as an afterthought and added as flat tones of flesh color. Ornate patterns of dress and costume were drawn with precise lines, and the subject sat or stood, rigid and bright against a plain, unadorned dark background. Just as sharp, clear-cut lines were the essence of their building, so were clarity and line the outstanding features of their painting.

They admired painting in much the same way they regarded poetry, prose, and even music—without aesthetic appreciation but in the practical terms of good craftsmanship and the artist's ability to recreate the sitter's likeness and personality. Although inspired by court painters, the Puritan portraits avoided the finery of the British royalty and aristocracy. Puritan custom frowned on display of excessive ornamentation, the ostentation of gold, silver, lace, or buttons, and the depiction of frivolous activity. Consequently their images showed severe, hard-shaped groups of unsmiling people, with grim, unchangeable seriousness of purpose.

The first Puritan painters were called "limners," a word derived and abbreviated from the Gothic "illuminator," showing that Americans tended to abbreviate the long words from the very beginning. An illuminator is one who makes images or pictures in manuscripts or books. The first limners were sign painters, men who decorated coffins or ornamented coaches with coats of arms. They sought to increase their income with portrait commissions from the few colonial personalities who were important enough to have their likenesses made. They were the only artists in the colonies.

Although most limners are unknown to us today—there are names without paintings and paintings without names—their works, which were hidden away in attics and dusty back rooms of museums for many years, have recently gained in prominence. Great value is attached to them and, after centuries, they are suddenly in demand, commanding fantastically high prices in the art market. They are important not only in terms of American his-

This portrait of Ann Pollard, by an unknown limner, typifies the two-dimensionality and linear quality of early American painting. COURTESY MASSACHUSETTS HISTORICAL SOCIETY

tory and antiquity. Because of their two-dimensionality, linear quality, lack of reality and decorative surface patterns—all dominant qualities of modern painting—they are also important in terms of the history of American art.

Although the Puritan tradition caused considerable similarity in the choice and handling of the subject—all were depicted in folk style with dummy likenesses and with a sameness of design in which the subject was isolated on the canvas with little or no background detail—the quality and style of limner portraits were as varied as the full time professions and training of the artists. Most limners had very little, if any, formal training in art. Their professions, however, varied widely. By 1690, seven limners, each with another business in addition to portrait painting, were active in Boston, a city of eight thousand inhabitants.

"Self-Portrait" by Captain Thomas Smith. WORCESTER ART MUSEUM

One of the best technicians among them was a sea captain, Thomas Smith. His self-portrait, in which he posed in a stance similar to Dürer's famed self-portrait, tells us that, at the very least, he was familiar with that great artist's work as well as with Holbein's. Captain Smith sits with a very untypical open window behind him, through which can be seen a sea battle in which he was undoubtedly a participant. His hand rests on a grisly human skull, more appropriate for a gravestone than a portrait, that sits on a paper neatly inscribed with his own verse, perhaps with reference to the sinking ship seen over his shoulder: "Why should I the World be minding, / Therein a World of Evils Finding, / Farewell thy Jarres thy Joies thy Toies thy Wiles thy Warrs."

From 1700 onward, the burgeoning spirit of confidence and assurance that was being expressed in business expansion, trade,

This portrait of Caleb Heathcote, c. 1710, is attributed to the Pierpont Limner. COURTESY OF THE NEW YORK HISTORICAL SOCIETY, NEW YORK CITY

and new settlements throughout the colonies was reflected in the portraits by the limners. No longer was the work of Holbein the only guiding spirit. The vivacious court paintings of Anthony Vandyke executed during the first half of the seventeenth century were now setting the style. Vandyke, the finest pupil of Peter Paul Rubens, left his Flemish home and his position as chief assistant to the great Dutch master to move to London, where he soon attained topmost standing in the royal court and created the style that became the essence of English painting for the century that followed.

Sophistication, ease, relaxation define these later limner portraits. As the Holbein-type line was softened, a Vandyke-type modeling of features was emphasized. Color grew richer, postures more graceful, faces became tender and softer, more an echo of the prosperity and ease of the present than of the rockbound rigors of the beginnings. Flamboyant and florid background settings indicated the new sense of aristocracy and wealth that was becoming so vital an influence in the colonies. Nevertheless, the American stamp—the stress on good likeness, the unrelenting clarity of features, the no-flattery, no-compromise-with-truth school of portraiture, the untrained and unpolished brushwork and paint handling—prevailed at all times. Practicality was still far more important than aesthetics.

Nearly a century after the landing on Plymouth Rock one New Englander summed up the Puritan attitude toward art: "It's more noble to be employed in serving and supplying the necessities of others, than merely in pleasing the fancy of any. The Plow-man that raiseth Grain, is more serviceable to mankind, than the Painter who draws only to please the Eye. The Carpenter who builds the good House to defend us from Wind and Weather, is more serviceable than the curious Carver, who employs his Art to please the Fancy."

The practical architectural solidity remained in these later limner portraits, despite the façade of newfound sophistication. Somehow, regardless of the Vandyke influence on color, detail, background, features, and expression, the American portrayed by the limner was a Yankee, as stalwart and solid as the timbers of the wilderness that had fallen before his ax.

Then, as new generations peopled the colonies, as population swelled to 200,000 in 1688 and to more than 1,500,000 in 1750, the Puritan was replaced by the Yankee. Still shrewd and resourceful, but without the dynamic Reformation-inspired fanaticism that had fired his grandparents' theological beliefs, the Yankee came into being. The Yankee was a New Englander and a native American, no longer an Englishman or a pilgrim or a colonist.

And it was Cotton Mather, the most famed of all the Puritan hellfire and brimstone preachers, who first used the word "American" to describe, not the Indians, but the descendants of the Europeans who comprised his parish.

In 1780 John Adams wrote, "I must study politics and war, that my sons may have liberty to study mathematics and philosophy, geography, natural history, and naval architecture, navigation, commerce and agriculture in order to give their children a right to study painting, poetry, music, architecture, statuary, tapestry and porcelain."

He was speaking for the hardworking, practical Americans who were used to dragging themselves up by the bootstraps and doing things the hard way, and for the millions of immigrants who were to fill the steerages of thousands of ships en route to America during the coming centuries—men who were willing to consider first things first and wait for their culture and comforts. He was not speaking for aristocratic Europeans who had grown up in an atmosphere of painting, statuary, tapestries, and all the rest of John Adams' better things, who, lacking the native born American's patience, wanted what they were used to when they wanted it.

Almost a century before John Adams voiced his credo of culture

Detail. Interior of an elegant eighteenth-century American home. COURTESY, HENRY FRANCIS DU PONT WINTERTHUR MUSEUM

THE ELEGANT COLONIALS

for the grandchildren, in 1684 to be exact, the Massachusetts charter was annulled and the first royal governor arrived in Boston. He was followed almost immediately by scores of wealthy, educated Englishmen, here for official and commercial reasons. No Puritans, these royal officials and tradesmen wanted what they wanted when they wanted it, which was immediately. They were the grandchildren for whom earlier ancestors had studied politics and war. They wanted houses much like the houses they had left behind in England; their impatience for comfort and desire for immediate luxury had a profound impact on the building and architecture of the eighteenth century. No simple, practical, Puritan homes for them!

When the eighteenth century dawned, 300,000 people lived in the New World. At the signing of the Declaration of Independence seventy-six years later, the population had boomed to 3,000,-000. And prosperity and economic growth had boomed right along with the population. A wealthy middle class grew wealthier as trade with England and the West Indies increased. England took all the raw materials the colonies could produce and shipped back all the manufactured goods the growing population demanded. Trade required more ships, and in remarkably short order a vast shipbuilding industry had developed in New England. Wealth poured into the seaport towns with a resultant rise in living standards. Soon, older generation Americans as well as the more recent aristocratic imports were demanding homes more indicative of their financial means; comforts, luxuries and the trappings of the better life. The sons of the merchants were soon fancying the daughters of the officials, and weddings were uniting them. The tastes and desires of both groups were solidifying into a positive identity as American gentlefolk, no longer English colonials.

To the English the word "colonial" meant inferior. To overcome this stigma and gain status, the wealthy classes sought to establish a new kind of aristocracy, through election to government councils and by acquiring lands by the hundreds of acres. These new aristocrats had coats of arms designed for themselves in England, and wealth replaced birthright as the doorway to society. All at once the self-made man, the Puritan-inspired ideal was moving upward on the social ladder into and beyond the class his grandfathers had migrated from England to escape.

Trade with England led logically to the opening of shops devoted to expanding and profiting from that trade. All sorts of imported manufactured merchandise—lace, silk, satin, furniture, wall hangings, jewelry, snuffboxes, weapons, buckles, watches, clocks, mirrors, wallpaper, books—were offered to and bought by a product-hungry public. The New Englander was a reader, a constant customer for books. And among the new books imported from England were important architectural studies of classical and Georgian styles which soon influenced building throughout the colonies. The colonial Georgian style evolved from the English architect Inigo Jones, who introduced to England the formal style of Italy that had been developed by the great Italian Renaissance architect Palladio. The most influential architect to work in his style was Sir Christopher Wren, who designed the magnificent St. Paul's Cathedral in London, as well as numerous palaces for royalty and mansions for the expanding middle class. James Gibbs was another English architect who had considerable influence on eighteenth-century colonial construction. What Englishmen called classical were the shapes and details they had borrowed from the Italians who had borrowed them from the Romans who had borrowed them from the Greeks. Soon the Americans were going one step further by borrowing them from the English and adding their own innovations to suit their time, place, and materials.

By the mid-eighteenth century Puritan fanaticism had burned itself out. Just as books had earlier led to the spread of Puritanism among the colonies, now books were spreading secular instead of spiritual ideas, and architectural books were causing Americans to look with dissatisfaction upon the design of their simple, practical, and rugged Cape Cod and saltbox homes. Puritan rigidity was being modified by new ways of seeing, new demands for merchandise, and more relaxed and versatile techniques as the colonial world began to catch up with the elegance Europe had known for centuries.

The beginning of the century saw Boston, New York, Albany, and Philadelphia taking shape as crowded urban centers. While the seventeenth century had reflected rural England, the culture of the eighteeth century was predominantly urban. London set the standards for art, architecture, literature, home furnishings, dress, and even social conduct. In New England the villages were becoming standardized. There were broad main streets divided into spacious lots for the meetinghouse and homes so no man crowded his neighbor; there were pastures nearby and convenient places for grazing cattle, for fruit and vegetable gardens, and even burial places for the dead. But as the small Puritan communities—the compact theological cells that had formed the nucleus of America—grew in population, their logical areas and arrangements grew crowded and the villages were shattered by their own expansion. Even as the post-World War II generation moved to the suburbs, people in those times moved out into the surrounding countryside to farm new land and build new homes. The escape from physical proximity diminished the influence of Puritanism, followed by a relaxation of the rigid codes of morality, behavior, and decorum of the pilgrim fathers.

As increased trade with England and the West Indies and new trade with China and the Northwest coast brought even greater wealth and prosperity, Americans developed a sense of the world beyond colonialism and Great Britain, and stirrings of commercial and even political independence were felt in the land. New homes, furnishings, paintings—all reflected this new affluent society. Commercialism and widespread wealth caused a questioning of the religious righteousness of the tight-knit Puritan group, and traveling merchants, journeying beyond Puritan towns, discovered that other people were neither Satanic nor necessarily evil—only human—and there wasn't really anything so bad about that.

A new eighteenth-century skepticism and intellectual humanism grew and became too powerful and universal for even the

Puritan citadel of New England to withstand, and a new taste came into being that was sure, sane, and refined. Despite their wealth and independence, this new aristocracy of shipbuilders, shipowners, ship captains, and merchants did not seek the usual "new-rich" vulgar or ostentatious. Instead, true to their quiet tradition, they filled New England's towns with charming, trim, elegant homes of brick, stone, and wood, detailed in advance from the best books of architectural plans available. They enhanced their homes with colonial reproductions of the famed English furniture makers, Chippendale, Hepplewhite, and Sheraton. Many of them favored the Windsor chair, with its refined shape and delicately turned supports. It was their money that supplied the wherewithal for the sparkling white churches that soon towered above the towns, churches as rich and lavish as the former meetinghouses had been crude and plain.

By the first quarter of the century important centers of colonial life were giving patronage to artists with known names and personalities—artists who meditated even upon abstract subjects and sometimes rendered works of art that were more concerned with aesthetics than with cold, hard practicality. Portraits were in great demand by colonists, both for home decoration and to be sent back as gifts to relatives in England.

Between 1725 and 1750, New England witnessed a growing specialization of occupations. It had become a commonwealth of shopkeepers, skilled mechanics, innkeepers, printers, shipbuilders, carpenters, and masons, as well as farmers, fishermen, and parsons. Builders, trained in the elegant Georgian style of Sir Christopher Wren, either in England before their arrival in America or here by English trained tutors, were active throughout the land. Taste and art were governed by English fashions and guided by English books. England's favored materials, however, stone and brick, were replaced with American materials, brick and wood, with stone used sparingly, if at all. The earliest New England examples of elegant homes strove mightily to imitate in wood the stone structures of England. Later, American builders modified the forms to fit the materials at hand, just as they modified the English plans to fit the climate and conditions of the New World.

In the visual arts—architecture, paintings, crafts—we can sense a growing independence, a gradual breaking away from established English traditions that culminated in the Revolution. Colonial craftsmen, like Paul Revere, made silverware as handsome as any that could be imported from England, and long rifles were crafted, as beautiful as any that could be imported, but far more accurate and deadly. "The most fatal widow and orphan makers in the world," the British called them.

Several important factors contributed to this growth and the attitudes that led to rebellion. Religion no longer dominated every waking moment of the majority of Americans. There was other work to be done. In a nation founded by deeply religious Puritans, there were, by the eighteenth century, many Americans completely indifferent to any form of organized religion, scorning even the ceremony of baptism. By 1776 when the zeal for political independence was at its height, church attendance was at the lowest point in America's history with only one church for every nine hundred people. By comparison, in 1939 there was one church for every five hundred Americans.

However, almost as a counterbalance, those who did cling to the church did so with an intensity that equaled that of the original Puritans. The "Great Awakening" of the 1740s and 1750s saw a zealousness that was little short of hysteria and religious ecstasy. By calling for hellfire and damnation, preachers such as Wesley, Edwards, and Whitefield hoped to awaken a consciousness of sin in what they felt was a sinful secular world. Whether they succeeded is still open to question. What was awakened in America after 1740 was a consciousness of the American spirit as distinct, separate, and different from Europe and a passionate belief in a separate and an independent destiny.

In 1732 a guidebook was published in the colonies which told of the "Flying Machine," a coach which could carry a traveler from New York to Philadelphia, a distance of one hundred miles, in the incredibly short span of two days. By 1750 a postal system was operating efficiently throughout the colonies so that a man in Massachusetts could find out and be concerned with what was happening in Virginia. By 1750 the standard of living of the thirteen colonies was higher than that of any comparable area in the world. Wealth was accumulating, not only in the coffers of the rich, but even more so in the pockets of the middle class. The colonist did an amazing amount of traveling, up and down the coast and overseas to Europe. Benjamin Franklin was only the son of a Boston tallow chandler, yet he managed to get a substantial part of his education abroad.

Architects were thinking in terms of town planning and paintings and painters were in great demand. An aristocracy of colonial government officials was firmly entrenched, with rich southern planters and equally wealthy northern merchants holding political control and acting as the center of America's artistic, literary, and intellectual life. The ambitious middle-class craftsmen, artisans, and professionals made up the bulk of the population. The poor, many of them former indentured servants—farmers who had already started the movement toward the western frontiers, fishermen, and low-wage earners in the growing cities— made up the third class. And at the bottom of the heap were the indentured servants, who were the surplus of England's prisons, and the slaves—a full fifth of colonial society.

Philadelphia surpassed all other American ports, and by 1750 it was the largest city in the colonies, second in size only to London in the entire British Empire.

Boston was the key city of the north, an area primarily involved with trade and manufacture. Possibly because of the proximity of Harvard many men of learning and letters gathered at Cambridge, and across the river Boston became a center of political activity, witty conversations, sedition against the crown, and the good, gay life. Concerts were held weekly. The free and easy manners of the Court of St. James in London were emulated to such an extent that Harvard students were often attacked in print as being too frivolous and luxury-minded, too given to drunkenness, idleness, and profanity ever to come to any good end.

Virginia was the main colony of the south, an area primarily concerned with large landholdings and agriculture. One of the most populous and extensive of all of England's colonies, Virginia was known as the home of brave and gallant men, fair women, horse racing, fox hunting, six-horse coaches, ten-gallon punch bowls, and estates that rivaled England's medieval palaces in their multi-gabled splendor. The Tidewater region, a lacy network of inlets and rivers, was the home of Virginia's aristocracy. Plantations were built close to the banks of the navigable rivers and streams down which some planters shipped their tobacco directly to the docks and mercantile establishments of London. There was no urban life, just harbors and plantations. Williamsburg was the seat of the colony's government, but it was never a bustling city.

Tobacco was the crop on which the eminence of Williamsburg and the prosperity of the Virginia colony were founded. Little else was grown and financial success was wholly dependent on Negro slavery. The large landholders of Virginia—the Carters, the Lees, the Byrds—grew rich from land speculation and tobacco, not from inheritances, and they took their cultural tastes from books and trips to London.

The governor, who sat at the top of Virginia's social ladder, kept his court and dominated his assemblies at Williamsburg, which housed not only the Assembly and the House of Burgesses but William and Mary College and a school for social dancing. The city attracted artisans, cabinetmakers, silversmiths, acting companies, and concert artists.

When British officers rode through Virginia in 1781 on their way to surrender at Yorktown, they must have marveled at the great Georgian homes they saw. These homes (the style was named for two of England's kings, George I and George II) were for the most part designed by their owners who not only conceived the houses and selected the plans, but hired the builders, measured, dictated, and supervised each step of the construction.

Georgian houses are distinguished by their Renaissance characteristics of perfect balance and symmetry. The exterior was usually austere and dignified with little embellishment, in sharp contrast to the rich, decorative interior.

The side limits of a typical early Georgian house were strongly defined. It presented an image of weight and solidity through the use of quoins—patterns of alternating stones that run from ground to roof—or wood designed to simulate stone, or pilasters (attached columns). Chimneys, impressive in size and large enough to take care of the many fireplaces needed to heat the house, flanked the bulk of the building. The windows, with eighteen to twenty-four panes and carefully framed to set them off from the surface of the wall, were large enough to provide abundant light to the interior, and were placed in perfectly symmetrical order on the building's façade.

The house sat on a high foundation surrounding a full basement. The main entrance, the chief architectural feature, usually atop a wide flight of stairs, gave the well-balanced exterior an air of genteel formality. A semicircular window above the doorway served as exterior decoration and provided light for the entrance hallway. The doorheads were often arched. In many cases triangular pediments or arches above the windows and elaborate doorways surmounted with pediments and framed between pilasters gave the house its classical character. Well-modeled cornices enriched the eaves. Roofs were hipped, sometimes truncated, and often broken with dormers topped by narrow triangular pediments. Sometimes the roof ridge would be flattened to form a deck. A dignified balustrade enclosing the deck was usually the crowning feature of the house.

Even more than the exteriors, the interiors reflected the newly found wealth and elegance of eighteenth-century colonial life. Classical elements, rich and often elaborate in finish and workmanship, were the keynote. As one entered through the front door, beyond the entrance was the high-ceilinged center hall, with its handsome staircase enhanced with a decorative balustrade and a molded and polished mahogany rail that would sweep gracefully into a turned post at the bottom. On either side were the rooms, most with paneled walls, though many were painted or papered. No longer were the structural beams and framing timbers exposed, now they were hidden behind plaster and paneling. Floors were of hardwood, perhaps parquet, or painted with decorative borders and centerpieces. Fireplaces, no longer used for cooking, were smaller than in seventeenth-century homes and were often faced with marble or tile. Over the mantle there was a large panel, a proper place to hang a portrait of the owner of the house. Over-all, the room's architecture provided a quiet and elegant setting for the display of rich furniture, glittering crystal and glass, and handsome textiles produced in New England's mills.

In essence, the difference between New England's seventeenth-century houses and the eighteenth-century Georgian houses was the difference between folk art and classical. Folk art is the happy result of what happens when an unskilled craftsman designs artifacts to fit his circumstances and materials. Classical art follows formally planned rules of design set down during the Italian Renaissance with no allowance for the accidental.

The elegance of eighteenth-century colonial life was reflected in stately architecture and handsome furnishings. COURTESY, HENRY FRANCIS DU PONT WINTERTHUR MUSEUM

The Georgian style appeared in the South about twenty-five years earlier than it did in New England, possibly because New England's traditions were more deeply ingrained. It appealed to the shipping magnates of seaport towns who earned their great fortunes in the overseas trade. The decks on the houses' roofs became known as "widow's walks," because from this high vantage point the wife of a sea captain could keep her lonesome vigil while awaiting her husband's return.

Regional differences of the Georgian style were relatively few. Georgian houses, whether in New England, the Middle Colonies, or the South were quite alike, differing only according to use, climate, conditions of living, available materials, and the owner's whim. Seventeenth-century houses were far more distinctive to their own particular areas.

Christ Church in Boston, built in 1723 and based on Christopher Wren's St. James in Picadilly, was the first example of classical building in the New World and led to the Georgian popularity. Designed by William Price, a local print seller turned craftsman, it had the tall spire, classical façade, and white color so typical of the eighteenth-century churches that still enhance New England today.

Louis Sullivan, the famous nineteenth-century Chicago architect, said, "What people are within, buildings express without." And indeed, the people who lived within the comfortable, charming, and elegant Georgian homes were as different as their homes were from their Puritan grandparents' houses. Painters of this period tell us in portraits far more eloquently than with words about these men and women who created our institutions and guaranteed our freedoms. Self-assured and confident, they posed relaxed and graceful against lovely landscape settings, Grecian columns, and velvet draperies, all symbolic of wealth and social position. The luxuriousness of their clothing and dress make it apparent they were more successful and sophisticated than the earlier colonists who posed for the limners.

An abundance of money in the colonies attracted many restless and ambitious artists in Europe who had not achieved the success they felt they deserved. None of them was a major artist, and many were hardly more than ambitious amateurs, but they did bring some skill and knowledge and an increasing awareness of the glamorous style of Vandyke which they passed along to the local practitioners. What these new artistic settlers hadn't developed in training, experience, finesse, and polish at home, they learned by doing and copying in the colonies. Their methods, techniques, and attitudes were, for the most part, self-taught and patterned very strongly on England's most popular society painters. American painting of this period, therefore, was primarily emulation and improvisation, as was Georgian architecture, of forms and styles generated and perfected in England.

These American paintings can be readily distinguished from their English counterparts through their more linear treatment which restricts modeling and roundness of form, sharp and precise outlines with no blurring of edges, and a general flattening of the figure. American artists painted people as they saw them, freshly and directly, without glamorization, and with an honesty that could have been painful to a sensitive sitter. Often, because of the artist's inability to paint with anatomical accuracy, a skill acquired only by disciplined and intensive study, there would be a disproportion of head to body. Arms and legs would have a bluntness of position and a peculiar angularity because of imprecise handling of depth and perspective and the artist's inability to foreshorten. And hands, always most difficult to paint, would invariably be hidden. The American artists did not follow the conventional methods and tricks of the more fluent Europeans in rendering drapery, form, and lights and darks. These were all things that had to be taught or learned through trial and error, and without teachers the Americans were all trying—and making their full share of errors. However, these artists did have great concern and ability for details of fashion in dress and design, which were always meticulously rendered, and from them we get unquestioned knowledge of how the colonists dressed and looked.

Many painters supplemented their incomes by opening art sup-

Portrait of Sir William Pepperrell
by John Smibert, ESSEX INSTITUTE,
SALEM, MASSACHUSETTS

ply stores where they sold paints, brushes, frames, and prints. Others worked as sign and house painters. The earlier pattern of the businessman who was a part-time painter had reversed itself. Now the full-time painter had become a part-time businessman.

Typical of the American painters of this period was John Smibert, who rose from obscure poverty to great wealth and renown. A dyer's son from Edinburgh who studied painting in Italy, he came to Boston in 1729 at the age of forty after a most undistinguished career in London painting gentlemen's coaches. Within one year of his arrival he had set up what was probably the first art show in America and was accepting portrait commissions from Boston's Back Bay patricians. He married an heiress and settled in one of the city's finest houses. However, despite his marriage and the honors that were heaped on him, John Smibert had to supplement his income with trade. He opened a wholesale-, retail art supply shop and imported engravings and casts of Renaissance works, and thus, as the art historian Alexander Elliot writes, "Scattered the fragments of a great tradition in new soil."

The self-made man was both the dream and the reality of the American, and colonial painters took pride in being self-taught. In American art, the transition from self-taught craftsman to full-time professional was as valid as the log-cabin-to-White-House saga—an unquestioned truth, unique in world history.

One of the first native Americans to feel Smibert's influence, and to develop skills far beyond his master's, was Robert Feke. Almost nothing is known of Feke, an enigmatic and mysterious figure, beyond the description passed along by a Scottish tourist. He had "exactly the phiz of a painter, having a long pale face, sharp nose, large eyes—with which he looked upon you steadfastly—long curled black hair, a delicate white hand, and long fingers."

He painted in the period between 1741 and 1750 in Boston, Newport, and Philadelphia, but beyond that his life is conjectural. Stories of travel and adventure cling to his memory, but they have never been documented. Somehow, in the strong self-portrait he left behind and in the aura of drama that surrounds his life, he represents the adventurous spirit of the times—the clipper ships, the traders, the daring voyages to far-off places.

Without formal training, Feke learned the rudiments of painting primarily through the study and copy of prints of contemporary and past pictures, and by long hours of perusal of illustrations in English books. His color was bright and bold, his brush strokes free and spontaneous, his pictures defined by sweep and dash. His men were handsome, reserved, and austere, his women seductive but distant. His subjects, the aristocratic ideal of colonial America, stand in landscapes, lean on classic columns, and enjoy the shade of ivy-covered grottoes. His style is distinguished by his concern for textures and costumes; the use of a heavy impasto, a most sophisticated mixture of white paints directly on the can-

This portrait of an unknown woman by Robert Feke typifies the artist's concern for texture and costume. COURTESY OF THE BROOKLYN MUSEUM

vas; and a coloristic quality that make his paintings unique for their time.

A portrait of General Samuel Waldo is one of his finest paintings. Sharply outlined, the general dominates the space with a proud and confident air. The landscape behind him is deep, spacious, and attractive. The general's features are portrayed with dignity and directness, and true to the American idiom, neither idealization nor glamour is anywhere evident.

Another of the great artists of the time, and possibly the most gifted silversmith in the colonies, was Paul Revere, a man who did far more for his country than simply risk a broken neck on

This silver bowl is an exquisite example of the craftsmanship of Paul Revere. COURTESY, MUSEUM OF FINE ARTS, BOSTON. BEQUEST OF PAULINE REVERE THAYER

a wild midnight ride. His most famous creation is a punch bowl of classic purity of shape. He fashioned it in 1768 during a high pitch of political activity, and on it he etched a dedication to the House of Representatives of Massachusetts Bay which, "undaunted by the insolent Menaces of the Villains in Power . . . voted NOT TO RESCIND." Revere was also a political cartoonist who painted a famed propaganda picture of the Boston Massacre. He printed currency, cast cannons, and ran a gunpowder mill to supply Washington's army with munitions. After the Revolution he went into the metal business, making church bells, copper boilers for the first steamboats on the Hudson River, and copper sheeting for the Boston Statehouse roof.

The silversmith was important to the colonies as more than an artist. In a country that had no banks, silverware was a form of economic security, and in the homes of the wealthy there were huge collections of silverware crafted in America but as handsome and as valuable as anything made in England.

Like many other American artists who followed him, Paul Revere aspired to be more than a mere craftsman. He was a man who played a heroic role outside his workshop and studio.

The first American sculpture beyond household tools and artifacts, weather vanes and gravestones consisted of ship prow carvings. Placed under the bowsprit they were the symbols of the ship. They served no practical purpose, yet hardly an American ship ever left its home berth for far-off ports without one. They became a sign both of affection and of superstition, even becoming, in some cases when they improved the appearance of ships, a matter of national pride. They were both unique and varied, with full figures well over life-size. They ranged in theme from national heroes to sculptured portraits of the owner or his wife, figures from mythology and literature, and even sea serpents and other legendary creatures. The most characteristic carving was a voluptuous female lunging forward with arms outstretched, head held high, eyes gazing steadfastly ahead scanning the distant horizon. Pine was the wood most commonly used, and it was painted and gilded. The figureheads were made in several pieces which were doweled together so that arms and other appurtenances could be removed in rough seas.

By the late nineteenth century with the popularity of steamships the figureheads went out of style, decorations were reduced to painted symbols and the boat's name, and a good part of the romance of going down to the sea in ships was lost to America.

[3]

THOSE
WHO
LEFT
AND
THOSE
WHO
STAYED

—**A** boy who got his first colors from the Indians and his first paintbrush from the tail of a cat . . .

—the close personal friend of King George III . . .

—the president of England's Royal Academy of Art . . .

—the man who painted America's great historical classics—"Death of Wolfe" and "Penn's Treaty with the Indians"—in England . . .

—the American artist called by Lord Byron "Europe's worst and England's best . . ."

—the first of a long line of American art students who left their native soil to study the great masters in the lands of their origin . . .

Benjamin West was all this and also the man who did more than any other to formulate the style of American painting after the Revolutionary War.

If ever any artist could truly be called "fortune's child," that artist was Benjamin West. Born in 1738, he was the tenth child of the keeper of an inn that still stands on what is now the campus of Swarthmore Col-

Detail from "The Death of Wolfe" by Benjamin West. THE NATIONAL GALLERY OF CANADA, OTTOWA. CANADIAN WAR MEMORIALS COLLECTION

lege, in a pastoral and virtuous Quaker community near Philadelphia. Friendly Indians taught him to mix the yellow and red
earth they used to paint their faces, and his mother provided blue
from her indigo dye vat. According to stories West told later,
the family cat supplied the hair of her tail for his first brush, and
he was in the painting business. That was at age seven. At thirteen he was accepting and carrying out commissions; at seventeen,
before he learned how to spell, he was accepted as an honorary
student at Benjamin Franklin's College of Philadelphia; at twenty,
a group of wealthy merchants of Philadelphia pooled enough
money to finance his art education in Europe.

"It is a pity such a genius should be cramped for want of a
little cash," one of them said, making him the first of a long line
of American art students who sought in Europe the artistic fountains from which the great masters flowed.

At twenty-one he was in Rome. He stayed there for three years
studying the Renaissance masters while deploring with Quaker
virtue the Italian emphasis on sensuousness and maintaining art
should elevate the mind rather than merely delight the eye. At
twenty-four he was in London, a popular prophet of neoclassicism, which was increasingly the rage of the time, and a close
personal friend of King George III. In 1768 he was active in
founding the Royal Academy of Art with Sir Joshua Reynolds,
becoming the second president of the academy in 1792 after Reynolds' retirement. In 1772 he was appointed royal painter of historical pieces, and he received patronage from the king for the
next thirty years. Although he never returned to America, he
remained loyal to his native country. When the colonies revolted,
despite his friendship for the king and royal patronage, his out-
spoken sympathies were with the Americans.

His home was a great mansion, a personal gallery—and his
friends and admirers were legion. He was certain of his talent,
artistic competency, and his high place in the history of art. He
was cool, assured, unruffled, confident. After forty years of married life his wife is reported to have said that she had never seen
him either intoxicated or in a passion. While most of West's con-

"The Death of Wolfe" by *Benjamin West*. THE NATIONAL GALLERY OF
CANADA, OTTAWA. CANADIAN WAR MEMORIALS COLLECTION

temporaries agreed with his self-appraisal of passionless greatness,
Lord Byron saw better things ahead for art. ". . . the dotard
West," he wrote. "Europe's worst daub, poor England's best."

Regardless of where he stands today as a painter, West helped
shape European and American taste, from his first successes in
London until his death in 1820. He built the first bridge of art
between Europe and America and exerted wide influence, not
only through the Royal Academy, but through the openhanded
and generous aid he extended to numerous American artists.
Indeed, almost every American painter who reached maturity
during those years felt West's influence in some degree. He was
admired and praised by his students, not only as a painter and
teacher but as a sympathetic human being. As the first successful
American artist in Europe, he served as a magnet to attract others.
His house was always filled with Americans who flocked to his

studio and home for help, advice, and employment. Generous almost to a fault, he handed out the coveted role of assistant in his grandiose painting commissions to several American students.

His studio housed a collection of originals and prints of famous works and a vast library of books on ancient art, literature, history, and art theory. His own work was based on that of previous artists and sculptors, and he collected examples of theoreticians reaching as far back as the Athenians.

There were no public galleries during West's time, but his studio and home served as a gallery and school for many young artists. Almost every important American painter of the late eighteenth century visited or studied with West, among them John Copley, Charles W. Peale—and a generation later his son, Rembrandt Peale—Gilbert Stuart, Matthew Pratt, Abraham Delancy, Ralph Earl, John Trumbull, and Henry Benbrigge.

He encouraged his students and exposed them to the traditions and aesthetics of classical forms. He assisted them in finances—in short, he threw open the gateway through which American artists passed in their search for the polished academic manner of the Europeans. He opened new dimensions in art to the descendants of the limners and loosened the bonds of Puritanism with the revelation of new color combinations, techniques, and pictorial means. The impact of Benjamin West on American art was profound and lasting. Indeed, he was the master who established American painting on its own secure footing on its own native soil—not through his painting, but through the gifts and abilities he passed on to others.

As for Benjamin West's own paintings, they gradually slipped into obscurity. Lord Byron's withering comment had accurately foretold the changing tastes in art.

—A timid boy who stayed at home and drew pictures to avoid the toughs of his neighborhood . . .

—a successful young man at the age of nineteen, ridden with guilt because, unlike the other busy Puritan citizens of Boston who were involved in manual labor or business, he spent seemingly idle hours in contemplation before an empty canvas . . .

—the son-in-law of the man whose tea was thrown into Boston harbor . . .

—an artist who set up a tent on the lawn at Buckingham Palace at the invitation of the king and sold admissions to 60,000 people to see a painting . . .

—an American portrait master who became an associate of the Royal Academy of Great Britain and is listed in the *Encyclopaedia Britannica* as an "English historical painter" . . .

John Singleton Copley was all this and the first truly great American painter as well.

Benjamin West and John Singleton Copley were born in the same year, 1738. Copley's parents were English. They had recently arrived in America and settled in Boston when he was born. His father, possibly a sailor, died in the West Indies shortly after his birth, and his mother, in order to support herself, operated a tobacco shop which was frequented mostly by sailors off the boats tied up at the nearby wharves. It was a tough and rowdy neighborhood, and the tobacco shop was surrounded by bars and cafes where the sailors drank and caroused. Small, plump, solemn, tightfisted, and timid, the boy stayed close to his home and mother and drew pictures to keep himself occupied and out of reach of the bullyboys of the neighborhood.

Things improved a little after his mother married a mediocre mezzotint artist and dancing teacher, Peter Pelham—not sufficiently to make her give up the tobacco shop but enough for them to move away from the frightening wharves and drunken sailors. Copley's new stepfather, trained in England as a portrait painter, introduced the boy to the stock poses and background props and, through prints and engravings, gave him a superficial acquaintance with the work of the European masters. Together they visited the studios of semiprofessional working artists of Boston. But Copley's training was painfully inadequate. In 1751, when Copley was thirteen, Pelham died. With little money left from his stepfather's will, Copley became a workingman in order to help support his mother and half brother. He set himself up in the business he knew best—printing, engraving, and portrait painting. In the language of baseball, in his first season he was the league's most valuable player. Before ten years had passed he was painting better pictures than any produced in America before his time, and better than most that have been painted since.

By the time he was nineteen, his portrayal of well-dressed, jeweled sitters gracefully relaxed within elaborate settings brought him great fame. A leading citizen of Nova Scotia invited him to Halifax with a promised commission to paint all the leading citizens of the city. But Copley was so terrified of travel that he refused this lucrative assignment and remained in Boston.

The old Puritan maxim that a wasted minute is a wasted dollar had not been lost on Copley. He was always plagued by a sense of guilt because, unlike other Puritan citizens who were busily involved with manual labor or business, he spent much of his time in his studio, seemingly idle, in what he considered practically useless contemplation before an empty canvas. Brought to task by a selectman for strolling on the Sabbath—the only recorded incident of Copley's doing anything against propriety—he soberly explained that he worked so hard and so long all week that he needed the Sunday walk for his health.

He had always been disturbed that unlike the art students of Europe, to whom a wealth of museums was available, he had never been able to study directly the works of the old masters. With remorse he wrote how he suffered from this handicap, this misfortune to be self-taught and never to have seen a first-rate painting while he was a young man. To compensate for his lack of early education and training he set himself constant problems, multiplying his technical difficulties, painting complex compositions, diverse textures, tedious color reflections. He ignored the static, posed formula by catching a model surprised in the act of rising from a chair, or leaning back in deep concentration while composing a letter. His sketchbooks were crammed with studies of human bones and muscles at a time when Boston morality forbade the nude model. More than likely, as some critics say, his achievement was due as much to hard work as to genius.

When Copley read that artists often worked in pastels, he wrote to the leading pastelist of Europe, Jean Étienne Liotard, a Swiss artist famed for thin, sentimental pictures, and asked him for a set of pastels, since none were available in the colonies. He did not expect to sell pastel paintings. But he worked freely and experimentally with them, and the qualities he achieved—airiness, lightness, and softness of color—undoubtedly had great influence on his oil paintings.

The French and Indian War brought economic depression to New England, and the flow of commissions for large oil portraits stopped. Copley tried to maintain his income by doing low-priced watercolor miniatures on ivory and on small pieces of copper, but he discovered that they took too many hours for the dollars they returned. Copley felt the feared pinch of poverty, but he tightened his belt and sought vainly for new large commissions. With the end of the war, prosperity flooded back to Boston. Before long Copley's studio was overflowing with the city's leading citizens clamoring for portraits. There was hardly a member of New England's upper class who did not sit for him, and there were more commissions than he had time to paint. Never one to overlook an honest dollar, he found ways to speed up production by drafting his half brother, Henry Pelham, to paint the backgrounds. And if sometimes the heads of his portraits seem too large for their bodies, that was because he often painted his bodies from dummies, so that the patron only had to sit for head and hands. But regardless, whether from sitter or dummy, his figures had a solidity unmatched by any other colonial painter. His sophisticated use of smoothly-laid-on, cool, metallic colors—greens, tans, russets, and grays—gave his work a power that was rarely equaled in America until the time of Eakins. Before he had reached the age of twenty-five, Copley had achieved his mature style.

Not until after he had moved to Europe and studied the masters did he appreciate the benefits of making preliminary drawings rather than working directly on the canvas and feeling his way with infinite care and a great deal of trial and error. The son of one of his patrons wrote, "Copley painted a very beautiful head of my mother, who told me that she had sat to him fifteen or sixteen times. Six hours at a time! And that once she had been sitting to him for many hours when he left the room for a few minutes . . . she had the curiosity to peep at the picture and it was all rubbed out."

In 1766, at the age of twenty-seven, he sent a painting of his half brother to an exhibition at the Society of Artists of Great Britain in London. He asked Sir Joshua Reynolds and the American expatriate Benjamin West, with whom he had had many years of correspondence, for criticism of the work, entitled "Boy with a Squirrel." Lavish in their praise, both men suggested that Copley would gain greatly from study in Europe. Reynolds wrote, "You would be a valuable acquisition to the Art and one of the first Painters in the World, provided you could receive these Aids before it was too Late in Life, and before your Manners and Taste were corrupted or fixed by working in your little way at Boston."

Copley wrote back, acknowledging the acclaim, saying gratefully to Benjamin West that approval of his painting from one "from whom America receives the same lustre that Italy does from her Titian or Raphael" was gratifying indeed. The words were most gracious, especially in view of the fact that Copley had probably never seen a painting or even a print by either of the Renaissance Italians, nor had he ever seen a painting by Benjamin West.

Despite the lavishness of his praise, Sir Joshua Reynolds and other academic artists of London felt that the "Boy with a Squirrel" was too hard, too linear, too detailed in its drawing, and too cold in its use of color, and consequently wanting in atmosphere. But they did elect him to the Society of Artists. West urged him to come to London and offered to take him in and introduce him to the important people of London. But Copley hesitated. He feared the loss of his financial security, he feared the bandits whom he was certain infested Europe, and more than

Portrait of Paul Revere by John Singleton Copley. COURTESY,
MUSEUM OF FINE ARTS, BOSTON. GIFT OF THE REVERE FAMILY

anything else he feared the ocean voyage, all no doubt reflections
of his early impressionable years on the Boston wharves.

For seven more years he remained in Boston, growing rapidly
wealthy. In 1769 he married the daughter of a rich Tory merchant, Richard Clark, bought himself a twenty-acre farm with
three houses on a magnificent site on what is now Beacon Hill,
and moved in next door to the showplace mansion of John Han-
cock, one of the richest men in the city.

Because of his timidity he never had a close friend. His only
close relationships were with members of his family. Nor did he
talk with the sitters who posed in his studio. He believed that
the proper Bostonians looked down on him, considering his art
menial, and that they were too ignorant to appreciate his work,

or even to differentiate between a good and a bad painting. So long as the likeness to the sitter was accurate, they were satisfied. Illusionism was indeed their only basis of evaluation, and Copley resented it deeply. A loner, he never had a pupil during his entire career, except for his half brother, Henry Pelham.

After his marriage he worked up sufficient courage to make his initial long journey, to New York, where he stayed for six months in the furious activity of painting New York's wealthiest citizens. With his courage mounting almost to the point of foolhardiness, he embarked on a farther voyage, to Philadelphia. This was one of the great moments of his life, his first viewing of attributions and copies of the old masters—authenticated originals were rare in the colonies. On his return trip he stopped at New Brunswick, New Jersey, and studied several portraits attributed to Vandyke.

Possibly it was this trip and the stimulation of seeing works from which he knew he could gain knowledge that gave him the necessary push toward England. Whatever it was, he finally decided to heed the advice of Benjamin West who had continued writing and urging him to come to the mother country. But the politics from which he had tried to remain aloof interfered. "Political events are neither pleasing to the artist nor advantageous to the art itself," he is reported to have told Paul Revere when he painted that great patriot's portrait in 1765.

Despite the fact that his wife and father-in-law were Tories, Copley, possibly because of his humble beginnings, had remained a Whig. His father-in-law, as agent of the East India Company, had imported some tea in December of 1773, and the day after the shipment arrived in Boston the patriots assembled in Old South Church to plan their action. With acquaintances on both sides of the thorny political fence and seeing something of right in each side, Copley tried his fine artist's hand at mediating the dispute. He was a far more accomplished painter than mediator.

The patriots demanded that the tea be returned without payment of duty. The merchants who owned the ships were vehemently opposed because, according to English law, if this happened the ships could be confiscated. Copley, fearful that force would breed more force, met with the merchants who had bought the tea, hoping to halt an outbreak of violence between the Whigs and the Tories. For fifteen days they argued, with neither side giving an inch, until finally the patriots, at the end of their tether of patience, dressed themselves as Mohawk Indians and in quite orderly fashion boarded the ships and dumped the tea into the harbor, thus igniting the fuse of revolution.

Copley, suspected by the patriots of having consorted with the Tories, set sail posthaste for England, leaving his wife and daughter to follow almost two years later.

According to art historian Alexander Elliot, "Not half his life had yet run, and most of his worldly triumphs lay ahead; but Copley's chief work was done. He left behind him in America a magnificent portrait gallery that would last as long as paint holds to canvas."

True to his word, Benjamin West saw to it that Copley was well received in London. He met Sir Joshua Reynolds and other members of the Society of Artists. What most impressed him was that students worked from a nude model—an experience totally unknown and forbidden to colonial Puritans. Now, thirty-six years old, he immersed himself in the world of art. He traveled to the continent, visited the great museums of Italy, Germany, and France, and drank in the treasures of the masters. Returning to London, he was elected an associate of the Royal Academy, but during the turbulent years of revolution he had few commissions and much time to absorb the theories of West and Reynolds. In the first portraits he painted in his London studio, there was a masterful synthesis of all these new influences with his own self-taught native skills. Almost at once he began showing new powers of color harmony and new techniques and subtleties.

In 1778, Brook Watson, a London merchant who was later to become lord mayor of London, commissioned Copley to paint a scene from his adventurous younger years, when he had lost a leg to a shark in Havana Harbor. "Brook Watson and the Shark" was a complete breakaway from Copley's portraiture to the epic historic and romantic themes which would constitute his major

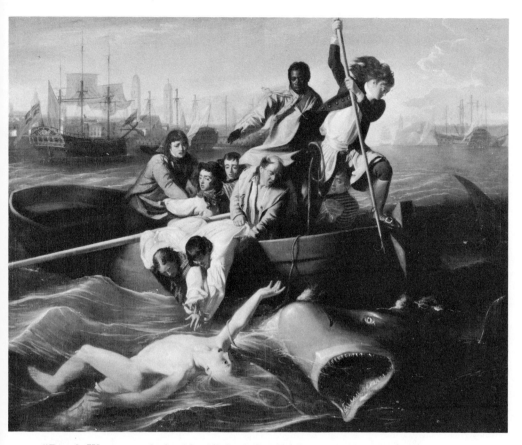

"Brook Watson and the Shark" by John Singleton Copley. COURTESY,
MUSEUM OF FINE ARTS, BOSTON. GIFT, MRS. GEORGE VON LENGERKE MEYER

work in England. Decades later the Romanticists of Paris painted
pictures of suffering, drama, and horror, but this painting, of a
man overboard, facing the savage jaws of death, stands alone as
the first horror painting of its age. There is reason to believe that
Géricault, whose "Raft of the Medusa" was painted in 1819, was
influenced by "Brook Watson and the Shark."

The "Death of Chatham," painted in 1781, which showed the
very moment that the elder Pitt, the Earl of Chatham, suffered
the stroke from which he later died, opened new and unique
financial opportunities for Copley. Taking advantage of vast
crowds that had gathered in London for the Royal Academy
Exhibition, he rented a hall in which to exhibit his oversized

painting and charged an admission to all viewers. More than 20,000 people paid Copley a 5,000-pound profit for the privilege. In Paris during the next century Courbet and other modern artists popularized the procedure. Never one to overlook a financial opportunity, Copley sold subscription rights, and 2,500 large engravings of the painting were distributed to subscribers.

Famous now as a historical painter, in 1781 he was commissioned to paint the "Death of Major Pierson" and the "Repulsion of the Floating Batteries at Gibraltar." The latter, a huge 25-by-20-foot canvas, took years to complete. To satisfy his intense concern for accuracy, Copley traveled to Hannover, Germany, to study and draw the German faces he needed in the picture. When finally completed in 1791, the painting was too large to exhibit in a museum, gallery, or hall. Never daunted, the artist pitched a huge tent in Green Park and proceeded to sell tickets of admission. Business boomed until neighbors, objecting to the noise of the crowds, forced him to move. The tent went up several more times and came down just as fast because of complaining Londoners, until King George invited him to pitch his tent and exhibit his painting in the garden of Buckingham Palace. The king, queen, and royal family viewed the painting and voiced their enthusiasm; 60,000 Londoners bought tickets and followed them into Copley's canvas culture palace.

Well known throughout England, Copley was now besieged by portrait commissions, but he grew homesick for Boston and generally discontent with his newfound fame. His friendship with Benjamin West deteriorated over the years, and he suffered from the sneers, jealousies, and criticisms of rival practitioners in his highly competitive profession. Two daughters born in England died, his wife grew melancholy, and he became obsessed with fears of poverty in his old age.

In 1795 he sold his property on Beacon Hill for three times his original purchase price. While busy congratulating himself for a handsome profit and a shrewd Yankee deal, he discovered that the land was destined to be the site of Massachusetts' Statehouse and consequently worth far more than he had been paid.

Portrait of Colonels Hugo and Schleppengull by John Singleton Copley. COURTESY OF FOGG ART MUSEUM. GIFT OF MRS. GORDON DEXTER

Screaming "Foul!" Copley immediately dispatched his son to Boston with a letter to Sam Adams, New England's top rebel, whose flinty portrait Copley had painted twenty-odd years earlier. He wondered, ". . . if you still retain any remembrance of Mr. Copley, who once had the honour of your acquaintance." Whether or not Sam Adams remembered is immaterial. The price remained as agreed.

Business recession, war, the Irish Rebellion, all took their financial toll. His lucrative patronage had now become an elusive trickle. On several occasions he teetered on the brink of poverty only to be snatched back in time by fortuitous commissions. He suffered from bad health and unfortunate investments, and one commission for a family portrait of a well-to-do English merchant ended up in a famed court case when the merchant, who disliked the result, refused to pay the agreed price. The critics grew sour, the public abusive. A sick, sorrowful, unappreciated old man, Copley died in London at the age of seventy-seven, perhaps wondering if the whole second half of his life hadn't been one big tragic mistake.

The years have been kinder to Copley than his contemporaries were, and today he is ranked unquestionably among the greatest American artists. Many authorities consider his colonial portraits superior to his more sophisticated work in London, feeling that he exchanged his incredible natural vision and ability for the bag of tricks, glamour, polish, and bravura of the society painters of London.

In Boston he was the greatest, and he undoubtedly knew it. But in London he felt inferior to the well-trained Europeans, and, being a sensitive man, this sense of inferiority undoubtedly diminished his work just as it did so many other American expatriates who followed him. A sense of inferiority and a need for academic training has been a trait common to many American artists. It has led some to better work, greater effort, and increased talent. For others, such as Copley, it led to an exchange of one set of talents for another, and not necessarily to improvement.

Primarily a Yankee colonial and never really a sophisticated continental, Copley, unlike his European contemporaries, could not reconcile himself to the fact that a moral citizen could still be a full-time professional artist. Just as his New England Puritan forerunners had been professional carpenters, sign painters, and ship captains, Copley sought to supplement his income by clever commercial practices. He sold tickets. He licensed reproduction rights. At times he was busier with his commercial improvisations than he was with his painting. Although improvisation is one of the distinguishing and enduring traits of American art, in Copley's case it could have been his undoing.

The *Encyclopaedia Britannica* lists John Singleton Copley as an "English Historical Painter." Still, on the day King George III admitted to his Parliament that the United States of America was in fact a nation, Copley proudly painted an American flag into one of his pictures. He was the second of America's long, honored list of artistic expatriates and the first great American painter.

Like so many of the great men of his time, Charles Willson Peale started his career without status, money, or education. Only three years younger than West and Copley, he was a slow starter, a less appreciated artist during his time, but a far greater man. More than merely an artist, he was a craftsman, scientist, inventor, and the organizer and owner of the first museum in America. A man of vast abilities and vital appetites, he survived three wives, fathered seventeen children, and died at the age of eighty-six while actively courting a fourth bride.

His seamstress mother apprenticed him to an Annapolis saddlemaker at the age of twelve. At nineteen he opened his own saddle shop and expanded it into a watch repair, silversmith, and portrait painting studio. A group of Maryland businessmen, impressed with his talent, lent him their financial backing, and at the age of twenty-five they sent him to London to study with Benjamin West, who had come to England under similar conditions.

Two years later he returned home and soon moved to Philadelphia where he spent the remainder of his life. His reputation for being able to make an exact likeness soon filled his studio with patrons, including Colonel George Washington of Virginia, whom Peale was to paint from life on seven different occasions.

Before his trip to London, Peale had been much concerned with freedom. Now, with the clouds of revolution starting to gather, he designed flags for the military companies that were forming and experimented with gunpowder. In 1776 he joined up and was elected a first lieutenant in charge of eighty-one musketmen. He marched off to the battles of Trenton and Princeton equipped with a self-invented telescopic sight for his rifle and a kit full of paints. Through the cold winter at Valley Forge he painted miniature portraits on ivory for the soldiers to send back home as mementos. Using bed ticking for canvas, he painted the portraits of Washington, Lafayette, Nathanael Greene and other revolutionary leaders.

Despite his part in the Revolution, Peale was probably the first American pacifist to oppose war on humanist rather than religious grounds. All human violence, he argued, was abhorrent, cruel, and stupid. He opposed any form of killing, whether mandated by the government or not, even dueling, which was in vogue at the time. A duelist "stinks," he wrote, "as much while living as he would after four days of being shot."

He built a gallery to house his portraits of thirty Revolutionary War heroes and gave free admission to the public. But now, with his family growing at a rapid pace and with portrait commissions from Philadelphia's conservative businessmen reduced almost to the vanishing point because of his uncompromising radical political stand, he turned to the public for support, building a museum of natural history. His method of stuffing animals and arranging them in a lifelike setting backed by pictures of the natural environment was a hundred years ahead of its time, but he made it work and pay him a profit. Friends sent him many gifts. Benjamin Franklin sent the corpse of an Angora cat. George Washington sent pheasants that Lafayette had sent from France. Tigers, bats, cranes, poisonous snakes were delivered to the museum, and with the help of his family Peale prepared them for display. Eventually the museum contained more than 100,000 items. Included were a wax image of Peale himself, paintings, stuffed monkeys engaged in human activities, and a reconstructed mastodon that he had exhumed from the property of a New York State farmer and recorded in one of his paintings.

He invented a smokeless stove, set elk teeth into lead as dentures for George Washington, formed an artists' association and school called the Columbianum, and presented the first public art exhibition held in the United States. But his employment of nude models scandalized proper Philadelphians and resulted in the

"The Artist in His Museum" by *Charles Willson Peale.* COURTESY OF
THE PENNSYLVANIA ACADEMY OF THE FINE ARTS

closing of his school. Nevertheless, he went his merry way, painting, inventing, innovating. He was most interested in helping
others. "I am disposed to do all I can to make others happy," he
wrote, "and thus make myself so."

He strove for perfection in his paintings. "Mediocrity is scarcely
admissible in the art of painting," he wrote. "It must be perfect
in the representation or it is of no value. But if it can be rendered

"Staircase" by Charles Willson Peale. PHILADELPHIA MUSEUM OF ART

so well as to render it a perfect illusion, there is no price too high can well be set on such a picture." Perfect illusion, scientific realism, deception, to fool the eye were his goals. Indeed, in some cases he rendered paintings so realistically that he used them instead of three-dimensional museum displays with the public's hardly being aware of his deception. One of his most charming paintings, "Staircase," a picture portraying two of his sons climbing a staircase, he placed in a false doorway in his museum, with an actual projecting wooden step at the bottom to heighten the illusion. The painting was so convincing that legend has it

George Washington nodded to the boys as he passed the painting while entering the museum.

Rembrandt, Raphael, Titian were the names he gave to three of his sons in hopes they would turn to painting.

Rembrandt Peale picked up his brush with serious intent for the first time at the age of twelve and continued for the next sixty years. He studied in London with Benjamin West, as his father had, and later visited London and Paris where he exhibited his father's mastodon. He was a museum curator in Philadelphia and Baltimore, taught drawing in the Philadelphia public schools, and tried to have his name changed to the simpler but pretentious Rembrandt.

The climax of his career was "Court of the Dead," a 24-foot canvas painted in 1820 containing twenty-three figures. Friends and relatives served as models, and, in tribute to truth, Rembrandt painted his dead man from an actual corpse. "A great moral painting," he called it. "It is the demonstration of the science of painting applied to its noblest purpose—the expression of moral sentiment," done of course by "a native artist." The painting was sent on a thirteen-month tour accompanied by a pamphlet that explained the scene and actions of the figures. It was placed within a specially built structure and attracted 32,000 viewers who paid a total of nine thousand dollars to see it.

As in the case of other paintings of the time and others that would soon follow, Rembrandt Peale's "Court of the Dead" was beginning to make itself felt to the American public, not as art but as theatrical entertainment.

Rembrandt, who lacked his father's joyous, ebullient inventiveness, created paintings that were easier for the public to understand and was far more popular in his day than his father had been.

Titian Peale was better known as the illustrator of several scientific expeditions than as a painter. His career took him to South America and the South Seas. During the last years of his life he worked in the patent office producing drawings of new inventions.

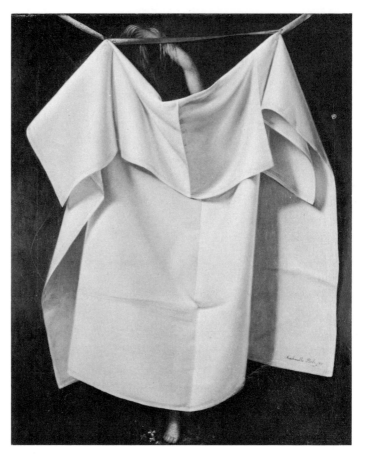

"After the Bath" by Raphael Peale. NELSON FUND, WILLIAM
ROCKHILL NELSON GALLERY OF ART, ATKINS MUSEUM OF FINE ARTS

Raphael Peale, the eldest son, made his most important con-
tributions to still life painting. He was a master of minute detail
and illusionism and delighted in the tricks he could perform
with pigment. Unlike his father, a teetotaler, Raphael was a
happy, habitual drinker who used his art to amuse and entertain
his friends and cronies. The story is that one day his wife saw on
his easel what appeared to be a painting of a nude covered with
one of her best napkins. Angrily grabbing for the cloth, her
fingers met only the painted canvas. While his wife blushed her
confusion, Raphael's friends roared with laughter.

"After the Bath," one of the finest still life paintings in history,
was painted, not as a serious work of art, but as a practical joke
on his wife by a henpecked husband.

4

The Revolutionary War not only severed the bonds of government between England and America, it cut the artistic and cultural ties that had existed since the time of the Puritans. In seeking new art forms to express their new independence, America's leaders, George Washington and Thomas Jefferson, found their source in the heritage of ancient Greece and Rome.

There was little building for more than a decade after the Revolution. Then, when buildings did rise to house the newly emerged nation's government, their inspiration was as old as man's yearning to be free, and they were as grandiose in style and scale as the philosophy and future of the Republic. Washington wanted a capitol expressive of Rome's austerity. Jefferson found his ideals in Greek democratic enlightenment. Under the spur of both great leaders a new style of "neoclassicism," or new classicism, referred to as the "federal style," arose and flourished between 1785 and 1820.

The United States was not alone in its admiration of Rome, nor was neoclassicism in America only an anti-English reaction. In 1763 the

Detail. The columns and pediment of the Capitol in Washington, D.C. typify neoclassic design

ROME, GREECE, AND WASHINGTON, D.C.

discovery of Pompeii unleashed an obsession for classical forms that swept throughout Europe as well as colonial America. The ancient Roman city had not been destroyed by the eruption of Mount Vesuvius, rather it had been covered with ashes, dust, and earth and sealed from view for over 1,700 years. The light of discovery revealed streets, houses, furnishings, sculpture, paintings, gardens, fountains, and the artifacts of Rome in all their classical splendor. A momentous discovery, it led to further exploration in southern Italy which resulted in the excavation of Herculaneum and Paestum. Fascination with the visual forms of the classical past brought about a corresponding interest in Rome's government, laws, culture, philosophies, and institutions—and led logically back to Greece and the democratic society of Athens. Indeed, the archaeologist's spade brought to life more than a long-dead city, it unleashed a new spirit of art that swept across the world.

Neoclassicism was not radically different from prerevolutionary forms but was a logical continuation of late Georgian style. Georgian had been based on classical forms of the Renaissance which had originated with the Romans and the Greeks, and the classical elements had grown increasingly prominent by the middle of the eighteenth century. Thus neoclassicism was easily grafted onto late Georgian structures. The stage had been set and the ground prepared. Neoclassicism grew in a nation both fertile and ready.

Some Americans found a parallel with the ancient Roman republic in more than art forms. They looked upon themselves as philosophical inheritors of the ancient Latins who had inhabited the hills of Rome prior to 500 B.C. and had established a republic by breaking the bondage imposed on them by the Etruscan kings —not unlike the Americans of 1776 who had thrown off the bonds of England's kings.

As the spirit of democracy flourished in the new republic, interest turned toward ancient Greece, especially, when at the turn of the nineteenth century the modern Greeks, as the Americans had, rose in revolt and fought for their own independence from the Turks. A revival of interest coupled with the development of Greek forms, often called the "Greek revival" emerged in America during the early decades of the nineteenth century.

More than four decades, from 1776 to 1820, marked the period of Roman dominance. After 1820 Greek influence shaped much of America's art and architecture.

Homes, mansions, and churches had been the hallmark of colonial architecture between 1620 and 1776. After 1776, with the establishment of independence, the emphasis shifted to administrative and public buildings and elaborate city plans. Instead of small homes, monumental civic structures were erected. The classical forms of ancient Rome, designed to accommodate great numbers of people, were ideally suited to the needs of the American republic. The colonial buildings of the eighteenth century appeared crude and barnlike and only superficial in their decoration. The forms of Rome expressed the pride, vigor, freedom, and democratic spirit of America, and they were defined in architecture by stately and dignified white civic buildings.

But just as earlier Americans had improvised on the European buildings they found in their builder's guides, Americans now combined Greek and Roman forms to forge an American style. Their sense of scale was Roman, but for details they turned to the Greek. Benjamin Latrobe, one of the designers of the national Capitol, used Greek detail in the Senate room and House building in 1817. The book *The Antiquities of Athens* by James Stuart and Nicholas Revett became a virtual daily reference book for America's architects who pored over its plates until gradually, by 1830, Greek details reigned supreme. Greek fashion became an American craze—in home furnishings, especially those designed by Duncan Phyfe, in women's dress and hair styles, and in architecture.

"It was in the Greek city-states," pro-Hellenists argued, "not in Imperial Rome, that liberty had flourished." Much as the Imperial British had burned the new Capitol and White House in Washington, D.C., during the War of 1812, so had the Romans ruthlessly eradicated the city-states of Greece. In the 1820s as the

The influence of classical Greek forms on early nineteenth-century American architecture and home furnishings is evident in this watercolor by Alexander Jackson Davis. COURTESY OF THE NEW YORK HISTORICAL SOCIETY, NEW YORK CITY

Greeks fought and died in their rebellion against Turkish rule, American sympathy was overwhelmingly and enthusiastically with them. Later, as passions cooled, Americans sought the beautiful serenity of Greek forms.

Another push toward Greek influence came from the fact that the Roman revival was associated with the Jeffersonian Republican Party, the "party of the people." Roman forms became symbolic of minimized federal autonomy and states' rights, and opposition to the tariff, a moneyed aristocracy, and class privileges. By the end of the War of 1812, Jefferson's political star was waning. The Federalists, representing the wealthy classes, were gaining power and favoring Greek style as a reaction against Jeffersonian democracy. In 1818 when designs were being considered for a building to house the United States Bank, the directors specified, "Grecian architecture in its purest form." The

Roman revival represented the art of the party to which the bank was a horror and a threat—and the bankers would have none of it.

The great age of the Greek revival spanned twenty years. It dominated the American scene from 1825 to 1845, as no other style before or since, and still remains a dominant theme in American architecture.

In the years after the Revolution many European architects joined the waves of westward migration. No longer interested in re-creating the environment of their home countries, they sought to create a new style that was totally American. But as in the past, it was not a professional architect or specialist in the arts who determined America's visual patterns. It was a traditional, many-faceted American, far better known as a statesman, philosopher, and President of the United States, Thomas Jefferson.

While he was ambassador to France in 1785, Thomas Jefferson had received an official letter from the governor of Virginia, requesting that he design the new state capitol, recently moved from Williamsburg to Richmond. Jefferson had seen the Maison Carrée, an ancient temple built during the height of the Roman Empire, and he had been overwhelmed by its beauty of proportion, perfection of detail, and fundamental simplicity. He had

The Capitol in Richmond, Virginia, designed by Thomas Jefferson.
COURTESY VIRGINIA CHAMBER OF COMMERCE. PHOTO BY PHIL FLOURNOY

always considered the American Georgian buildings at Williamsburg provincial, unimpressive, even crude and barnlike with "barbarous ornament," as compared to the glorious, majestic proportions of Rome's monumental structures. Thus, when he designed the capitol in Richmond in 1789, he modeled it along the lines of the Maison Carrée. The first grand neoclassic public structure in the United States, the style broke like an incoming flood tide across the length and breadth of the United States. In every city and state, neoclassic buildings emerged like mushrooms from the American soil—government buildings, libraries, schools, mansions—even hospitals.

Jefferson built his own home in the grand manner exemplified by Palladio, the sixteenth-century Venetian, whose architecture had been so influential in the development of the colonial Georgian style. The basic plan for Monticello was adapted from Palladio's Villa Rotunda in Vicenza. To this low central dome Jefferson added a colonnaded porch similar to those on the Pantheon in Rome. The octagonal side projections were his own innovation. And just as he had combined elements from various classical sources to create a home to suit his needs and interests, so later, in the planning of Richmond, he modified the capitol with two quite un-Roman stories necessitated by demands for office space.

The University of Virginia, the chief source of Jefferson's pride, served not only as a text on his Roman style but exemplified his ideals of a state-supported institution of education. The campus buildings were symmetrically planned with the complex dominated by the magnificent library, an exact replica of the Pantheon. Behind the library were homes for the faculty, each designed with different classical orders—Doric, Ionic, Corinthian. The whole complex blended together—buildings, gardens and site— in the open, spacious tradition of Rome.

In a letter to President Washington, Gouverneur Morris wrote, ". . . I think it of very great importance to our country to fix the taste properly, and I think your example will go very far in that respect. It is therefore my wish that everything about you should

A drawing depicting the symmetrically planned campus of the University of Virginia. COURTESY OF KENNETH M. NEWMAN, OLD PRINT SHOP

be substantially good and majestically plain, made to endure . . ." George Washington could very well have had this injunction in mind when he took upon himself the direction of the construction of the new Capitol.

A swampy site along the Potomac had been selected, and a French military engineer, Major Pierre Charles L'Enfant, was appointed to draft the plans. The location itself was a controversial subject. "A howling, malarious wilderness," some called it. "The Indian place . . . in the woods of the Potomac."

In its favor was the fact that it was almost midway in the long stretch of states, close to the thriving centers of Georgetown and Alexandria and accessible to transport both overland and by water. Mrs. John Adams, who was soon destined to move to Washington from Boston, called it, ". . . a beautiful spot, capable of any improvement."

L'Enfant, who had served under Washington in the Revolution, mapped the sites selected for the major buildings. Of the location of the Capitol itself, he wrote, "I could discover no one situation so advantageously to greet the congressional building . . . it stands as a pedestal waiting for a monument."

L'Enfant's plan was magnificent. A series of broad avenues radiated outward like the spokes of a wheel from the Capitol, the White House, and other important points. These main avenues were intersected with a grid plan of streets and blocks that ran directly north and south, thus combining the scope and beauty of Versailles, Paris, and other European cities with the efficient and orderly arrangement of American cities. The points at which the radiating avenues converged and intersected with other streets formed picturesque open squares, circles, and irregularly shaped blocks which were later enhanced with small parks, fountains, sculpture, and grassy plots, all with spacious views of the Capitol. All roads led to the Capitol which towers majestically above the city. Up to the present day city ordinances wisely prohibit nearby buildings from rising higher than the Capitol.

Architects were invited to submit plans for the Capitol, with an award of five hundred dollars plus a city lot offered for the winning design. Scores of designs poured in, but none was acceptable. After the deadline a young physician requested permission for a late submission, and when his belated plan arrived, its acceptance was joyous and immediate. "It captivated the eyes and judgment of all," Thomas Jefferson enthused.

"Grandeur, simplicity, and convenience seem to be well combined in this plan," George Washington announced.

The design had been developed by Dr. William Thornton, an English citizen born in the West Indies who was famed as a portrait painter, steamboat experimenter, and amateur architect. It was based on St. Peter's in Rome and St. Paul's in London—both structures embody classical Roman features and are crowned by monumental domes.

Building the Capitol was no easy task. Thornton immediately came into conflict with other architects who had their own ideas. The Frenchman Étienne Sulpice Hallet, better known to Americans as Stephen Hallette, was placed in charge of construction. In 1794 the clash of personalities became so intense that Hallette was dismissed and Thornton was given the building job. In 1803 Jefferson, then president, appointed Benjamin Latrobe to the job,

An early nineteenth-century picture of the Capitol in Washington, D.C., based on Benjamin Latrobe's original design. COURTESY OF KEN-NETH M. NEWMAN, OLD PRINT SHOP

and Jefferson took to the drawing board himself to design many of the details of the building. Jefferson was enthusiastic about Latrobe's work, but the legislators complained that acoustics were bad in the House chamber and demanded renovations. In 1814, the invading British, under Rear Admiral Sir George Cockburn, made renovation an absolute necessity by burning the Capitol down—along with most of the other public buildings in Washington, D.C.

Patriots claimed that the admiral entered the House chamber, took over the speaker's chair, and called out, "Shall this harbor of Yankee Democracy be burned?" and his troops roared "Aye!" Chairs, desks, and books were gathered into piles and set aflame, and the interior of the building was gutted. Destruction would have been complete except for a rainstorm that swept the city that night. The next day a violent windstorm blew up and completed the debacle.

Latrobe, who had been designing waterworks and steamboats in Louisiana, was called back to Washington to reconstruct the burned out Capitol. In 1817, after almost incessant conflicts with his political supervisors, he resigned to make way for Charles Bulfinch, a Boston architect and the first American artist to participate in the construction of the Capitol. Bulfinch completed the building much as Thornton and Latrobe had planned it. At long last, in 1824, the first gala reception was held in the rotunda to honor General Lafayette, the first foreign visitor to speak before a joint meeting of the Congress.

The vast emptiness of the walls of the new Capitol's rotunda was a challenge to tempt any artist. John Trumbull staked out his claim early and in strength—the support of Thomas Jefferson and the praise of George Washington. As president of the American Academy of Arts founded in 1808, he saw the rotunda as his own personal gallery and the American Revolution as his private painting preserve. To paint a national history series which would be the major art work of the era had been his ambition ever since he had become a serious artist. He spent years making the sketches of battlefields and portraits of important people of the period that he later incorporated into his paintings. He planned many paintings, but only four, all equally monumental in size and dullness, were finally installed in the rotunda.

According to legend, it was his sisters' needlework that attracted John Trumbull to art. His father, the governor of Connecticut, could not have been less enthusiastic. Painting was a trade for skilled laborers, not for male members of the New England aristocracy. Despite his father, John Trumbull became the first born gentleman to work as a professional painter in America.

John was shipped off to Harvard at the age of sixteen in the hope that school would take his mind off painting. However, once in Cambridge, he went calling on John Copley in nearby Boston for advice, and soon he was painting and copying all the works he could find. A letter from a tutor to John's father calling attention to the boy's "natural genius and disposition for limning" apparently had no influence on the father's attitude.

Trumbull's talent found a valuable outlet at the beginning of the Revolution. For a year and a half he served as a military map maker, and for a few weeks he was an aide-de-camp to General

Washington. Then, in a fit of pique because a commission making him a full colonel at the age of twenty was postdated for three months, he resigned from the army and barred himself from participating in the war, except with paint on canvas. "A soldier's honor," he informed Congress, "forbids the idea of giving up the least pretensions of rank."

He returned to Boston where he rented John Smibert's studio, with that artist's paintings still in place, and set himself up in the portrait business. London beckoned and in 1784 he made a pilgrimage to Benjamin West's studio. West encouraged him to paint but suggested that he confine his efforts to small pictures because of his visual handicap. (An accident during Trumbull's childhood had resulted in the loss of one eye.)

While in Europe he met Thomas Jefferson with whom he discussed his plan for the visual history of the Revolution. Jefferson was enthusiastic, but the only financial aid he could offer Trumbull was a job as his secretary. Trumbull refused the offer. In 1789 he returned to the United States, and for ten years he painted only in his spare time while working as a diplomat and business speculator. Then followed four years of professional disappointment as an artist in New York. More because of his business and social connections than his talent, he was elected an officer of the newly formed American Academy of Arts. Displaying eight small dramatic compositions that were studies for his murals, he attempted to finance the work by obtaining advance subscriptions, but without success. Four more years of toil were wasted in London during the War of 1812, and then in 1816 he returned to the United States to become elevated to the presidency of the American Academy of Arts.

After three years of deliberation, in 1817 Congress finally voted to commission Trumbull to paint four of his proposed twelve Revolutionary War subjects as murals for the rotunda of the reconstructed Capitol in Washington, D.C. And they were less than enthusiastic with the result. Few people shared Jefferson's opinion that all of Trumbull's paintings should be retained in America as "the nucleus of a national gallery and as monuments of the

taste as well as of the great Revolutionary scenes of our country."
John Quincy Adams wrote that he was not disappointed since his
expectations had been low to begin with. The small sketches on
which the murals were based reveal a genuine talent for narrative
painting, but the full fire and plasticity of his concepts were lost
in their transfer to large size. Or perhaps the years between the
sketches and the murals had taken their toll of his talents.

To gain critical approval Trumbull took the four paintings on
a tour of the nation's leading cities, and if they gained anything,
it was more faultfinding and critical barbs. Charles Willson Peale
found them monumentally dull. One government legislator complained that, although they cost the government $32,000, "they
were not worth even thirty-two cents!"

John Randolph, looking at the "Declaration of Independence,"
which contains forty-eight portraits, declared it was ". . . a shin-
piece. Never was there before such a collection of legs submitted
to the eyes of man."

After the installation of his murals, Trumbull suffered the bit-
terest disappointments of all. First, the government refused to
buy a collection on which he had worked for more than forty
years, and, secondly, the American Academy failed under his
presidency. Inept management, poor judgment, and misuse of
his position led to the organization's financial ruin. His first act
as president was to persuade the directors to purchase two of his
religious paintings for seven thousand dollars, together with several smaller pictures for lesser sums. The money was to have been
returned to the academy through admission fees paid by the public. But the public expressed little interest in seeing his work, and
eventually the paintings were back in Trumbull's possession and
the academy was teetering on the brink of bankruptcy.

Instead of providing necessary leadership to the new nation's
young painters, Trumbull had become a bitter and tyrannical old
man. Conflicts flared with the students and faculty at the academy—and just as he had resigned from the Revolution, now in
equal pique he stalked out of the academy. Samuel B. Morse took
over the presidency, and the aristocrat John Trumbull turned to

"Declaration of Independence" by John Trumbull. YALE UNIVERSITY ART GALLERY

business and the production of mediocre portraits to support himself during his final years.

The classic revival was most fully expressed in Horatio Greenough's monumental marble statue of George Washington—fifteen feet tall, twenty tons in weight. Greenough labored for nine years in a Florentine studio to bring forth a half-nude George Washington, bare to the waist, seated like Caesar on an ancient Roman throne. A drape thrown over one upraised arm covers the lower half of his figure, while his other arm grasps a spearlike scepter. Greenough's intent was to represent Washington, symbolically, as a man retired from the military service who has given up the sword and taken on the mantle of the lawgiver. With uplifted hand he proclaims his judgment. The statue was the perfect image of the President's face and features blended with the Roman past, from toga, sandals, and sword down to the accurately reproduced Roman throne.

But in 1843 neither the American public nor the Congress was ready to accept the "father of our country" as a half-naked Roman. Far ahead of its time in concept and vision, it ended up the butt of countless jokes and an expensive dust collector in the basement of the Smithsonian Institution, responsible for the discouragement of government patronage of the arts for almost one hundred years.

The hapless saga of the naked president started in 1832 when Greenough received a five-thousand-dollar commission from the Congress to create a monumental statue of Washington for the Capitol's rotunda. This was the first major sculptural commission to be awarded to a native-born American. He returned to Italy, where he had studied, to carry out his assignment, and there he absorbed the details of numerous statues of ancient Roman emperors before starting his own work.

Nine years later "Washington" crossed the Atlantic on a navy sloop at a cost of $7,700. It took another $5,000 to move it from the navy yard to the rotunda. By the time it was in place, the

Horatio   Greenough's   marble statue of George Washington aroused considerable controversy.
NATIONAL COLLECTION OF FINE ARTS, SMITHSONIAN INSTITUTION

government had paid out some $21,000 for its $5,000 statue. The figure was in perfect harmony with the Roman structure of the rotunda—as solid, durable and monumental as the Capitol building itself.

No sooner was the statue in place than the carping and criticism started. Greenough himself complained of poor lighting in the rotunda, and the public reaction was a roar of laughter. One wit wrote, ". . . Washington was too prudent, and careful of his health, to expose himself thus in a climate so uncertain as ours, to say nothing of the indecency of such an exposure."

For three years the figure sat in the rotunda, the object of a never-ending flow of gibes. Then Congress moved it to the more secluded west front of the Capitol, and from there to the east front where it stood under a makeshift shelter until 1908. Finally, in that year another $10,000 was appropriated to have it placed in the basement of the Smithsonian Institution. A generation later it was joined by the "Spirit of St. Louis," the plane Lindbergh piloted across the Atlantic, which was suspended from the ceiling. With the emergence of the space age, when the first sputnik landed, the "Spirit of St. Louis" was moved upstairs for better public viewing, but Washington still sits gathering dust in the basement.

According to one critic, Daniel M. Mendelowitz, "Today we are conscious of Greenough's vision. No American of his time had conceived of a national symbol of such heroic proportions, nor had thought in such monumental terms. The stately gesture and commanding pose represented a sculptural conception which in power and dignity went far beyond the topical and illustrational effects typical of the period."

Possibly it was the expense that discouraged Congress, or maybe it was the public's lack of understanding and appreciation. Whatever the reason, from 1843 onward Congress ceased appropriating money for commemorative statues of the nation's leaders. In fact, after Greenough, few if any congressional commissions went to artists until the Works Progress Administration project of the 1930s.

5

THE DREAMER, THE VISIONARY, AND THE INVENTOR

The philosophy of "The difficult we do immediately, the impossible takes a little longer" had served the colonies and young republic well. There came a time, however, when despite all the will, wanting, and confidence that American artists could muster, the impossible remained just that.

Washington Allston, John Vanderlyn, and Samuel Finley Breese Morse dreamed of reviving in America the splendors of the Renaissance by re-creating here the genius of Raphael, Michelangelo, and Titian. They saw themselves as the rootstock of American cultural immortality, the masters destined to glorify America's neoclassic age with gigantic historical canvases, inspiring allegories, and romantic, poetic reveries.

Unfortunately, none of the three ever developed his talent to the level of his aspirations, and even if he had, America was not ready to offer the opportunities that would make use of that talent. Occasional congressional appropriations were no substitute for the patronage of a sophisticated aristocracy, royalty, or church, especially in an increasingly

Detail. "The Old House of Representatives" by Samuel F. B. Morse. IN THE COLLECTION OF THE CORCORAN GALLERY OF ART, WASHINGTON, D.C.

Jacksonian Democratic society. While Allston, Vanderlyn, and Morse never came near the fulfillment of their dreams, they added European sophistication to American painting and proved that in American art there was room for more than Puritan practicality —that there was room for imagination, daring, and an inner eye that sees below the surface of reality.

Samuel Morse, who became totally disillusioned as a painter by the age of forty-one, turned his interests to electricity and ten years later perfected the telegraph. Of the three, Morse was the only one to achieve lasting fame—as an inventor, not as an artist.

Washington Allston was the leading American painter of his day and the first great romanticist painter of the United States, if not the world. His subjective paintings were done some twenty years before those of the distinguished French romanticists Géricault and Delacroix. Deeply intellectual, Allston realized very early that there was more to painting than objective reporting, more to life and art than merely what met the eye, that a world existed in the inner recesses of the mind, that faithfulness to nature and its objects—the ideal of America's eighteenth-century artists—left unanswered the questions raised by imagination, dreams, and visions. The historian Alexander Eliot wrote, ". . . the young Allston was alive to the romantic spirit of the coming era, and he set himself to painting subjective pictures, scenes appearing in his inner eye. This was at least as important a discovery for American art as, say, the Abstractionist Revolution which was to explode a century later."

Allston was a dreamer from the start. He was born on an ancestral plantation in South Carolina, and his earliest memories were of imaginative tales of ghosts and supernatural beings, told by the plantation's slaves. "I remember that I used to draw before I left Carolina at six years of age," he wrote. "My favorite amusement . . . was making little landscapes about the root of an old tree in the country," and "converting the forked stalks of wild ferns into little men and women, by winding about them different colored yarn."

Neither boarding school, Harvard University, nor drawing lessons from an unknown artist could change the dreamer to a realist. Upon graduation from Harvard he sold his share in the plantation for enough money to allow him to live, learn, and work for many years in Europe.

The treasures of the Louvre were a revelation. "Titian, Tintoretto, and Veronese absolutely enchanted me," he wrote to a friend describing the color, imagination, and sensuous appeal of these masters. But more important, he saw what he wanted to see. ". . . they took away all sense of subject . . . it was a poetry of color I felt . . . giving birth to a thousand things the eye cannot see." They addressed themselves, "not to the senses merely, as some have supposed, but through them to that region of the imagination which is supposed to be under the exclusive domination of music."

Music was one of the prime sources of inspiration in Allston's life. In another letter he wrote, "I have been more affected by music than I have ever been by either painting or poetry."

Allston's desire to paint great pictures in the tradition of the Renaissance masters, rather than merely good ones, led him to Rome—a far different Rome now than the city that had inspired the young Benjamin West. Artists were involved in a new classicism, based on the ordered compositions of the Renaissance and influenced by the works of the seventeenth-century landscape artists who lived and painted in Italy—Claude Lorrain and Nicolas Poussin. John Vanderlyn and the writers Washington Irving and Samuel T. Coleridge, friends from London, followed Allston to Rome, seeking the picturesque and romantic in their writing just as Allston and Vanderlyn sought it in their art.

In 1808 Allston returned to Boston, married, and lived and worked for three years in the same studio that had been John Smibert's. Unable to earn a living from his painting, he turned to portraiture. But his drawings and sketches and memories of Europe emerged to color his work, and he escaped the cold reality of Boston with warm recollections of southern Europe. "Coast Scene of the Mediterranean," painted between 1808 and

1811, carried him back, at least mentally, to the romantic places he loved. Finally, in 1811, unable to adjust to the puritanical atmosphere that still pervaded Boston, he took his family off to live in London, this time accompanied by a pupil, Samuel F. B. Morse. Allston remained in London for seven years, gathering praise, accolades, and cash awards for his romantic works, many of which were inspired by literary sources including myth, prophecy, and the Old Testament. "Uriel in the Sun" was awarded the first prize of 150 pounds at the British Institutions Exhibit. "Dead Man Restored to Life by the Bones of Elijah" won high acclaim and 200 guineas from the Royal Academy. And from Benjamin West, president of the Royal Academy, came the highest tribute of all when he said, "Allston has commenced where most of us leave off."

Perhaps if Washington Allston had accepted West's other words, that painters could not live by historical and classical painting alone and that only by selling themselves as fashionable painters of vacant faces could they attain financial success, Allston could have spared himself much heartbreak. In 1815 his wife died, and in 1818 he returned to the United States, even though the English pressured him to remain in London and elected him an associate of the Royal Academy. He brought with him an unfinished monumental painting, "Balthazzar's Feast," which he clearly intended to be his masterpiece. Despite his aspirations and the recognition heaped on him by critics and friends on both sides of the Atlantic, Allston never did learn to compose a group of figures properly, or even to draw the human figure adequately. His large compositions modeled after the works of the Renaissance masters were all failures, and no one understood this better than Allston himself. Until the end of his days he was haunted by advice he had once given a student: "A painter may be blessed with every gift of nature, but unless he has acquired the art of design he can never express himself. If you would not be tormented by a consciousness of having noble and beautiful conceptions to which you cannot give birth, you must give much of your time to drawing."

"Balthazzar's Feast" became more burden than blessing. And like the ancient mariner of his friend Coleridge, he carried it on his back like an albatross for the rest of his life. A group of American friends raised a fund to enable him to finish it, but try as he might it was beyond him. Finally, in desperation he completed a series of other paintings to repay his unhappy creditors and clear his clouding conscience.

He lived with his second wife in a studio-home in Cambridgeport, just across the river from Boston—a shadowy figure to all but his close friends, but known to them, despite his failures with the human form, as one of America's great masters. He was the first American to turn to imagination, flights of fancy, and poetical expression—an artist in tune with the cultural currents that were sweeping the new spirit of transcendentalism across New England. Together with his friends, Longfellow, Lowell, Emerson, Channing, and others, he realized that the rigors and struggles—the battle for survival—of the colonial seventeenth century were long since past and that a Utopia could lie ahead. These were years bursting with freedom of thought, soaring imagination, and poetic insights without bounds, and Washington Allston sought the immortality in art that Longfellow and Emerson gained in letters. Unfortunately his desire was greater than his talent.

Until his dying day, in sketch after sketch, he labored over "Balthazzar's Feast." The result was a mass of mediocre studies and a never-completed final canvas condemned by history as nothing more than a monumental and pretentious ruin.

Aaron Burr was John Vanderlyn's first patron. In art, as in politics, Burr had his own ideas. In 1796 he sent the sober young artist from Kingston, New York, to Paris instead of London for his training, and in the French capital Vanderlyn found himself under the overpowering influence of Jacques Louis David, the neoclassic master and director of the French Academy. Here he painted antique forms and classical images and rendered his figures with precise drawing and firm modeling, as though from marble statues rather than living flesh. He absorbed more than the French master's technique; he absorbed his philosophy that only studied historical canvases or classical allegories were worthy of a great artist's talents. Years later, when Aaron Burr was accused of treason, Vanderlyn repaid his patron's past generosity by helping to support Burr in Paris.

Vanderlyn became a close friend of Washington Allston, and together the two young men visited Rome, reinforcing each other's dream of an American Renaissance in which each would paint his noble visions on the walls of the numerous public buildings springing up in the new nation's burgeoning cities.

A grandiose classical painting, "Marius Musing amid the Ruins of Carthage," painted in Rome in 1806, was entered in the Paris Salon Show of 1808. Although the jury passed it without comment, the Emperor Napoleon was so taken with "Marius" he ordered it be awarded a medal—and almost overnight the American was a world-famed artistic celebrity.

He returned to America in 1815, confidently bearing with him the paintings Paris had admired, seeking fame in America to match his Parisian accolades—and congressional commissions to complete his Renaissance dreams.

Unfortunately he achieved neither.

America had little appreciation for the frozen classical postures of his "Marius," despite Napoleon's medal—and "Ariadne," a skillful nude that other Parisian painters had found most admirable, raised a storm of scandalized protest that hindered rather than helped Vanderlyn's career. The first sensual nude to be publicly displayed in America, "Ariadne" was denounced as an example of European depravity, and the Columbian Art Society went so far as to adopt a resolution against the display of such painted indecency.

As for Vanderlyn's Renaissance ambitions, John Trumbull had more influential friends, and the mural commissions for the Capitol's rotunda went to the Connecticut aristocrat.

Still undaunted, Vanderlyn unveiled a series of detailed perspective drawings which he intended to work up into an oil panorama. Friends and admirers raised enough money to con-

"Portrait of the Artist" by John Vanderlyn. THE METROPOLITAN MUSEUM
OF ART, BEQUEST OF ANN S. STEPHENS IN THE NAME OF HER MOTHER, MRS.
ANN S. STEPHENS, 1918

struct New York City's first art museum, a circular neoclassic
structure near City Hall. The Versailles panorama was painted
over a nine-year period and duly installed on the second floor
with smaller paintings occupying the walls of the main floor. An
admission fee was charged to pay for upkeep and maintenance of
the museum and to return a profit to the investors, but the public
was singularly disinterestd. Whatever else Versailles was, it wasn't
"show biz." Few customers came and the building was taken
over by creditors and eventually became one of the city's criminal
courts. The panorama was sent on tour to various cities, but the
hinterlands could work up no more excitement than New York,
and eventually Vanderlyn returned with it to his birthplace in

Kingston. It is now in the possession of the Metropolitan Museum of Art in New York.

Despite the Versailles failure, Vanderlyn painted successful panoramas in New Orleans and Havana. But for a man who sought to elevate the national taste, who had visions and ambitions far beyond the prosaic and dreams of greatness equal to Michelangelo and Raphael, success with panoramas was small reward, and the inability to realize his ambition made him a bitter and frustrated man. And as he aged, his talents shriveled with his fortunes.

The great opportunity for which he had hungered all his life finally arrived in 1838. After the death of Trumbull, Congress commissioned Vanderlyn to paint the "Landing of Columbus" for the rotunda. But the commission was too late. Even though Vanderlyn went to Paris to execute the work, he was unable to carry it through to completion. The mural, which was by no means a significant work of art, was finished by his assistants.

In 1843 when told of the death of Washington Allston, he wrote: "When I look back some five or six and thirty years since, when we were both in Rome together and next door neighbors on the Trinita del Monte, and in the spring of life, full of enthusiasm for our art, and fancying fair prospects awaiting us in after years, it is painful to reflect how far these hopes have been from being realized."

His own final years brought even more bitterness and frustration and a slow corrosion into obscurity. John Vanderlyn may have been the first American with sufficient courage and daring to challenge the nation's Puritan heritage with naked flesh, but it wasn't enough. As the art historian Daniel M. Mendelowitz wrote: "The circumstances of American life defeated Vanderlyn. His was one of the first and most noteworthy of the many nineteenth century artistic careers that came to naught because they were not based on a realistic estimate of American needs and tastes. . . . Equally important, America still had no great collections of paintings and sculpture which could nourish the artist . . . and sustain his faith in the validity of his dreams."

Past and future, practicality and dreams lived simultaneously in the mind and fought for the soul of Samuel Finley Breese Morse. Disappointed because the classical fifteenth-century past— and his dreams—were unattainable, Morse turned at an age "beyond which Raphael had accomplished all his wonders" to practicality and the future. He invented the telegraph and attained wealth and fame—and saw a statue of himself erected in New York City's Central Park.

While a student at Yale, Morse wrote to his father that, "My ambition is to rival the genius of a Raphael, a Michelangelo, or a Titian." His father, a practical, hard-bitten Yankee minister of the Congregational faith, aware of his son's idealistic attitude toward painting and his simultaneous interest and experimentation with electricity, wrote back: "Your natural disposition renders it proper for me earnestly to recommend to you to attend to one thing at a time."

The most important one thing at the time of his graduation in 1810 was painting. Gilbert Stuart and Washington Allston had seen young Morse's work, and as a result they encouraged his father to send him to England. In 1811 he accompanied Allston to London and was turned over to Benjamin West for schooling.

Classical training was fine, his practical mother wrote, but how did he expect to earn a living?

He answered: "My purpose is to elevate and refine public feeling by turning the thoughts of my countrymen from sensuality and luxury to intellectual pleasures." Painting could be purely intellectual, he believed, looking at art with his scientist's mind. "There is not a line or a touch in his [Benjamin West's] pictures which cannot be acounted for on philosophical principles. . . . I cannot be happy unless I am pursuing the intellectual branch of art. Portraits have none of it; landscape has some; but history has it wholly."

To which his mother replied with true New England foresight, "You must not expect to paint anything in this country for which you will receive any money to support you, but portraits."

Washington Allston, who heard in young Morse the echo of his own early dreams, wrote the elder Morses of how tragic it would be if an artist with Samuel's genius should "raise no higher superstructure than the fame of a portrait painter."

As if to prove the validity of his ambitions and to justify Allston's faith, Morse exhibited in the Royal Academy Exhibition of 1813 a small sculpture and a huge painting, both of a "Dying Hercules." The small clay figure from which the 48-square-foot canvas had been painted was awarded a gold medal, and a London critic listed the painting among the first dozen of the more than two thousand paintings on exhibit.

But despite critical acclaim, he could barely earn enough to pay the rent on his studio. Back home in Boston after four years abroad, he was given some small commissions for historical paintings, but the demand for these paintings was limited, and before long he was traveling throughout New England painting portraits for fifteen dollars a head. As the years passed his travels broadened, his reputation grew, and he found rich patronage for portraits of De Witt Clinton, James Monroe, and scores of other important people of the day. In 1825 the city of New York commissioned a portrait of Lafayette for the City Hall. Morse's full-length portrait of the old French general is among his best portraits. It is more than a practical likeness. Monumental and painterly, it has power, vigor, splendor, and a dramatic flavor of romantic intensity that presents the aging soldier-statesman as a symbolic hero image—a man of greatness in the sunset of life.

Morse still despised the work of portraiture. In 1832 he wrote from Paris, wondering, "Will my country ever employ me on works which will do it honor?" He had seen Rembrandt Peale's "Court of the Dead," and he longed to create his own monumental painting, one that he too could send on the road as a moneymaking traveling exhibition. He decided in 1821 to paint the House of Representatives in session in its neoclassic chamber, rendering a historical document that would be "a faithful representation of the national hall, with its furniture and business." The Congress allowed him to improvise a studio in the basement

"Lafayette at City Hall" by Samuel F. B. Morse. PHOTO BY TAYLOR & DULL, INC.

"The Old House of Representatives" by Samuel F. B. Morse. IN THE COLLECTION OF THE COR- CORAN GALLERY OF ART

of the Capitol, and all but one of the eighty-eight legislators ac- tually posed for their portraits.

He captured the moment during the evening session when the chamber's central chandelier was being lighted. The artificial il- lumination of the room presented problems, and the vast area dwarfed his figures. Still he used the mellow light to underplay the fact that the House was still being built, and he grouped the eighty-eight figures informally around and behind their desks

in a composition that gives great vitality and freedom to the painting despite its tremendous restrictions.

Shown in New York, New Haven, Boston, and elsewhere, the huge canvas was almost completely ignored by an indifferent public. A group of distinguished friends signed a pamphlet urging Congress to buy the painting, but the representatives were as cold to it as the public. After the painting's financial fiasco on tour it was finally purchased by an Englishman. Twenty-five years later it was discovered, cracked and dirty, nailed to a wooden partition in a New York City warehouse.

Morse labored over hated portraits for seven more years to get out of debt—and finally, backed by commissions for copies of paintings by Rubens, Rembrandt, and the School of Athens, he took off in 1829 for a three-year trip to France and Italy.

Out of this trip emerged his tour de force—an extraordinary effort that far surpassed anything attempted before in American art. It was Morse's final lunge for grandeur, his final effort to prove that an American could equal or surpass anything anyone else had ever done. "The Exhibition Gallery of the Louvre," executed in 1832 and 1833, though a financial failure as far as public exhibition was concerned, was a spectacular painting, as large in its artistic accomplishment as it was in its nine-by-six-foot size.

Morse' showed exactly how paintings were exhibited in the Louvre, from floor to ceiling, with little or no space between. Above all, he copied and reproduced the work of the most famed of the great masters—da Vinci, Titian, Raphael, Rubens, Veronese, Vandyke, Poussin—reducing them all to miniature scale, yet masterfully organizing them within a composition that included not only the hall and the masterpieces but other artists at work copying the paintings.

In 1832 he returned to New York, and though the public ignored him, his fellow artists heaped honors on him. He helped to found, and later headed, the National Academy, and while he labored once more over despised portraits, his friends took his case for a commission to decorate the national Capitol before Congress. But the commission went to John Trumbull.

"I have too long lived in the hope of doing something for the capitol," Morse wrote in his shattering disappointment. "I have studied and travelled to prepare myself, I have made sacrifices of feeling and pecuniary interests buoyed up with this phantom of hope which is daily growing dimmer and will soon vanish. . . . I see year after year the vigor of my life wasted in this vain expectation; Raphael had accomplished all his wonders and had died some years before my present age; a few more years and my fate in art is decided."

His fate in art was already decided. That year, at the age of forty-one, he abandoned his father's injunction to "attend to one thing at a time" and branched out into several fields of activity. He was appointed a professor of the arts of design at New York University, practiced daguerreotype, and began experimenting once more with electricity.

Ten years later, exactly twenty years after he had painted the House of Representatives, he sat in the same chamber and heard the bill passed authorizing his experimental telegraph. What must have been in his mind as he strung wires through the dust and rubble of the Capitol cellar to demonstrate his invention to Congress? Down there, where his studio had been, he discovered a cast of his small statue, his gold medal winner, "The Dying Hercules." Was it then, at the very dawn of his new world honor, that he began to compose in his mind the letter sent to his friend James Fenimore Cooper many years later?

"Alas," he wrote, "the very name of picture produces a sadness of heart I cannot describe. Painting has been a smiling mistress to many, but she has been a cruel jilt to me; I did not abandon her, she abandoned me. I have no wish to be remembered as a painter; my idea of that profession *was* perhaps too exalted; I may say, *is* too exalted. I leave it to others more worthy to fill the niches of art."

In 1844 the first telegraph message flashed over the forty-one miles of wire between Baltimore and Washington: "What hath God wrought?"

Possibly, until the end of his days—despite wealth, fame, leadership of the National Academy, a beautiful young wife, a career devoted to the promotion of his invention, and a fight to preserve his credit for it—he kept asking himself the same question and wondering if his life might not have been fuller and more gratifying if God had wrought for Samuel F. B. Morse his immortality as a painter.

[6]

DECADES OF THE COMMON MAN

In 1803 the Louisiana Territory was purchased from France for fifteen million dollars—for two and a half cents an acre—doubling the nation's size and removing whatever boundaries might have existed, even in man's imagination, to the westward surge of America. The Monroe Doctrine was a flexing of American muscles in 1823 at the kingdoms and empires of Europe and a proud warning against intervention in this hemisphere. Texas was annexed in 1845. Mexico was invaded a year later, and Great Britain came to terms over the northwest boundary. By 1848 the gold rush was on, southwestern California and the Oregon Territory were under the Stars and Stripes, and the United States stretched from the Atlantic to the Pacific, fulfilling the dreams of "Manifest Destiny."

The nation opened up. New states joined the Union. Industry soared and Congress grew. Between 1840 and 1860 population almost doubled to thirty-one million. Gold was on the bottom of the West's streams, needing only to be picked up. Farmland was available in scope and vastness

Detail. "Penn's Treaty with the Indians" by Benjamin West. COURTESY OF THE PENNSYLVANIA ACADEMY OF THE FINE ARTS

unimagined in the Old World, waiting only for the settler and his plow. Men were trudging gleefully across the forests, the plains, and the deserts, scrambling over mountains, fording and swimming rivers, exploring and exploiting a vast, almost uninhabited continent.

Whole new dimensions of history were unfolding. Napoleon's invasion of Egypt resulted in the deciphering of the Rosetta stone, and new secrets of the civilization of the Nile were unveiled. Mesopotamia was excavated. In Mexico, Mayan temples and ruins were explored. Europeans were becoming more involved with their own Middle Ages, finding that period, with its myths, mystery, and romance, more atractive than the harsh, violent present, or the cold, inhuman intellectualism of the classical periods.

As the nineteenth century unfolded, Europe's wars, tyrannies, and revolutions bred violence, despair, and pessimism. But America, exploding westward, was a bonanza, a Utopia—a land not only filled with promise for the common man, but a land that was making good on this promise.

Interest in the Middle Ages, in long-dead civilizations like the Egyptian and the Mayan stirred the imagination. But the unknown, the opening of this vast, new, strange, and exotic wilderness made real and attainable for the comon man what had heretofore only been an abstract philosophy—freedom, economic as well as political. This was something new, alive, vital, throbbing with excitement, spurring the imagination of Americans as it had never been spurred before.

The wars for independence in the United States and France had given the individual a new dignity and the right to express himself as a man. The philosophy that all men were created equal was a dramatic concept that strengthened man's belief in the validity of his own expression. His new ideas widened his interests and opened new vistas, and the Gothic Middle Ages vied with the frontier for his interest. Gothic was an age of romance, expressing deep human feelings, sometimes mystical and irrational, sometimes inspirational and subconscious. Eventually these concepts of romanticism and freedom, fed by both the new wilderness and the Middle Ages, broke through the academic discipline of classicism that controlled public taste to become the dominant artistic expression in the nineteenth century.

Romanticism stands in direct opposition to classicism, favoring feelings over reason, intuition and personal taste over tradition, and content over form. For inspiration, novelty, change, and a fresh source of stimulus, painters looked ahead to the wild exotic frontier, while architects turned back to the Middle Ages—both seeking the same fountainhead of romanticism.

The romantic novels of Cooper and Scott, the writings of Washington Irving, were opening minds and eyes to the beauties of nature and the excitement of imagination, both here and in Europe. The seeds of romanticism Washington Allston had sown had fallen on fertile ground. People were rebelling against the rigid strictures of classicism. The Greek-revival style might be appropriate for federal and public buildings and banks, but it wasn't a style the American family wanted to live with. For the man with calluses on his hands, the Greek revival was far too formal. Searching for something different, he filled the cities, the suburbs, and the habitable landscape with Gothic reproductions—Swiss chalets, Tudor cottages, and Tuscan villages.

The new Gothic style in architecture differed from that of the Greek and Roman revival in many ways, but primarily in its informality and profuse use of decoration. The emphasis on repose created by horizontal details and low roof lines of the neoclassical style was replaced by vertical accents. Classical columns, domes, vaults, and round arches gave way to pointed arches, clustered columns, ribbed vaulting, and buttresses. Sentiment and nostalgia constituted the mood of the day, and Gothic elements in architecture satisfied this mood.

Spires, towers, turrets, and pinnacles created an interesting, uneven silhouette against the skyline, while the battlements and projecting gargoyles brought to mind knights and fair ladies, dark castles and remote moors, romance and chivalry. The slim tracery of design in windows, flattened Tudor arches, and mossy stones were reminders of earlier days in Shakespeare's rural England, and high, narrow rooms, tall windows, stained glass all contributed to a mood of religious exaltation, mysticism, human warmth, and romantic nostalgia.

The taste for picturesque and irregular architecture worked hand in glove with the practical needs of the newly rich middle classes. Heretofore, symmetry rather than convenience had dictated the floor plan of a building. Now America's wealthy manufacturers and traders wanted rooms where they would be most useful, and classic design be damned! The housewife wanted her kitchen next to the dining room, not half a house away, and a man who liked to read in bed wanted his library close to the bedroom, not downstairs on another floor. Regardless of how the Greeks or Romans had lived, the new breed of Americans wanted to live in their own manner, and the Gothic style gave them freedom to innovate ingenious interior arrangements. Changed room plans resulted in greater variety of exteriors, and the uniformity of earlier days was replaced by individuality.

Andrew Jackson Downing, writer, architect, and landscape designer, was most influential in bringing about the romantic revival in architecture. He deplored the pomposity and pretentiousness of pseudo-Greek temples as homes for plebian middle-class Americans, and he called the rigid and formal eighteenth-century gardens that had been borrowed from England, along with the Georgian style of architecture, an affront to nature. His arguments on the subject of building materials read as if they were written in the latter half of the twentieth century.

"Stone," he said, "should be used in such a way as to bring out its natural beauty—and wood should be treated as wood, not marble." A building should fit its site, he insisted, and pseudo-Moorish castles had no place in the midst of modern cities, nor should a man with simple Christian tastes attempt to live in a castle designed for a barbarian emperor. The ideal house, he argued, should be designed for the needs of the owner and should be adapted from elements selected from various historical architectural styles, modified and constructed to suit the personality, needs, and tastes of the individual who would inhabit it.

Downing firmly believed that city dwellers would benefit from natural surroundings, and he fought to have tracts of land reserved for large parks within the boundaries of our modern cities. His advanced vision resulted in the creation of New York's Central Park, with its gently curved roads and walks, informal landscaping, outcroppings of rocks, lakes, pools, meadows, and lawns. His philosophy, similar to the Japanese, that landscape design should retain the feeling of nature, refined and softened by art, is the dominant principle in landscape architecture today.

The most successful builder of Gothic houses in nineteenth-century America was probably Alexander J. Davis. When Davis was sixty-four, he made a list of the various kinds of houses he had constructed over the years—American Log Cabin, Farm House, English Cottage, Lombard Italian, Collegiate Gothic, Manor House, French Suburban, Swiss Cottage, Tuscan from Pliny's villa at Ostia, Surburban Greek, Oriental, Moorish, and Castellated. His fame, however, rests mainly on the handsome Gothic mansions and great baronial estates built for people of newly acquired wealth. There were mazes of rooms, hallways, and staircases, topped by forests of towers, turrets, balconies, chimneys, and gables. To the person whose eyes were accustomed only to the severity of Georgian and neoclassic buildings, his houses were informal, charming, fresh, and vivacious. Tastes have changed and today they seem overembellished—but not without charm.

Tuscan villas were particularly popular. Many American artists, writers, and sculptors who went to Italy to work or study were attracted to the lovely houses that dotted the Tuscan landscape, and later re-created the design in an American setting. The style, with its bold contrasts, rectangular masses of warmly colored stone and stucco, and broad overhanging eaves, had great visual appeal, arousing interest and nostalgia for warmer and sunnier places than the cold gray north of Europe.

The work of Orson S. Fowler exemplifies American innovation and inventiveness in home design. Fowler criticized Downing for designing only for the upper classes. In a book entitled *Home for All* he presented his Octagonal House, which he claimed solved the problem of providing an inexpensive, practical home for the average American. His design did away with poorly lighted corners, saved steps between rooms, eliminated long hallways, provided a maximum amount of closed living space with a minimum of construction, and required less fuel to heat. The odd triangular spaces became closets and water tanks. His book became a best seller and went into seven printings. Octagonal Houses blossomed all over America, the first of a vast number of radical, offbeat, and oddball houses that would delight the adventurous and infuriate their more conservative neighbors.

By mid-century the popular Gothic, Tuscan, and other styles were being reflected in interior and furniture designs as well as in architecture. Rooms were once again paneled with wood as in colonial days, and all the pointed arches, carvings, designs, and exotic embellishments of the exteriors were adapted for use indoors. This elaborate use of Gothic detail for interior design reached its gaudy apex in steamboats, veritable palaces of pleasure, that plied America's rivers shortly before the Civil War.

While the variety of architectural styles had charm and vivacity, it led to a great decline in the design of functional furniture. Since little or no household furniture had been used in the Middle Ages, there were no authentic Gothic originals from which designs could be copied, except for altars and choir stalls, and these were hardly household items. A most grotesque assortment of impractical and uncomfortable chairs, beds, tables, and cupboards emerged. New mechanical lathes for shaping wood and jigsaws for cutting patterns had been developed, encouraging a flourishing of elaborate decoration. Furniture makers, freed from more time-consuming and expensive handicraft skills, went overboard experimenting with this machinery. Industrial growth had brought about more widespread prosperity; the cultured gentlefolk of the eighteenth century whose tastes were based on classicism were lost in the backwash of the surging new economy. As delicate, tasteful handicraftsmanship for an elite clientele gave way to machine production for mass consumption; elaborate ornamentation replaced simple elegance.

Benjamin West had dictated a single avenue to American artistic greatness—classical historical painting. He demanded stage-set groupings in which heroes of the past reenacted significant events. But West had not been an orthodox neoclassicist. He had portrayed great moments of modern history in modern costume. In his painting, William Penn and the Indians were clothed like colonials and aborigines—not like Roman senators and Middle European barbarians, which would have been the proper neoclassic way to do it. According to the proponents of neoclassicism, painting had but one purpose—to improve mankind. And mankind would be improved through intellect, not by appeal to crass emotions. Antiquity was the time-tested era of reason; therefore

"Penn's Treaty with the Indians" by Benjamin West. COURTESY OF THE PENNSYLVANIA ACADEMY OF THE FINE ARTS

Greek and Roman art styles were the only valid guides to subject matter and techniques. Knowledge would come, not from studying nature, but from the old masters. Anything contemporary was considered as dross, to be cleared away with cold reason, because the present implied impermanence. Originality was taboo. The purpose of the artist was not so much to be creative as to bring forth the glories of the past. Horatio Greenough had followed strict and accepted neoclassic rules when he carved his famed statue of George Washington for the Capitol rotunda.

Portraits were painted for money and were not considered worthy of being called art. Genre paintings, which portrayed the local and low-level life and provincial behavior of uneducated people, were beneath contempt. Still life was considered an exercise in technique rather than art, and since nonhuman nature could play no part in human enlightenment, landscape was considered at best a secondary kind of art. Neoclassicist painting was not supposed to appeal to the common man, its subjects were intended to make sense only to one whose education and cultural achievements made him familiar with the legend, myth, or historical event portrayed. Its reliance on intellect and abhorrence of emotion said that man was evil—and dangerous—unless controlled by those of superior breeding and intellect. In effect, neoclassicism was antidemocratic and denied the individualism which was so much a part of what the Revolution and the Jacksonian years had been all about.

Men who had explored and settled a whole new world were not about to accept the idea that only the lessons of the past were worthy—nor could they resist celebrating and portraying their newly won land and freedom. Instead of painting classical heroes of ancient history, they sought to portray the adventurous spirit of contemporary man, turning to the untrammeled frontier and the untamed beauty of the wilderness for subject matter and inspiration. Landscape became not only a patriotic symbol, but a way to express the deeply felt religious and romantic feelings of the age. For those who could no longer believe in a fundamental religion of unquestioned miracles and myths, the grandeur of nature symbolized the power of the Almighty. Romanticism, therefore, expressing the frontier philosophy, the rights, freedom, and dignity of man's own personal expression, became the mood of the times.

Influenced by the evocative descriptions of nature in Washington Irving's *Rip Van Winkle* and James Fenimore Cooper's *The Pioneers,* and by the writings of Emerson, Thoreau, Whittier, and Bryant, who practically painted the wilderness with words, many American artists began to paint landscapes. Some artists traveled west, following the pioneers. Others discovered Washington Irving's Hudson River, close to the eastern cities but still mostly uninhabited, untamed, and exotic. They created a spacious land on canvas, with deep tunneled-out areas and vast wild space.

Trumbull, Allston, Vanderlyn, Morse had looked eastward toward Europe and backward into time for their inspiration, and their dreams had been shattered by the unattainable. The artists of the next generation—Thomas Doughty, Thomas Cole, Asher Durand, John Kensett, and others, called the Hudson River School of painters—looked westward into America and the future. And painting for the many, rather than the few, they reached great heights of financial success. Though their critical and public acclaim did not live on into history, their work left a legacy that was a hymn to the land, its hills and rivers, its beauty and freedom and promise.

When Thomas Doughty began to record the scenic beauty of nature, he probably was not aware that landscape painting had never before supported an American artist. But he might have surmised that the literary climate both influenced and expressed public taste, and that affluent townspeople's affection for the rural, stimulated by nostalgia, would be backed up by purchase.

The son of a Philadelphia shipwright, Doughty had been apprenticed to a leather currier, and later owned his own leather shop. Color was an important part of the leather currying business, and he began using his colors to make pictures, which, to his surprise, sold faster and for better prices than his leather work. He studied for a while with the Philadelphia portraitist Thomas

Sully and found constant and growing success selling landscape paintings to the new urbanites of Baltimore and Boston and the cities in between. He was probably the first American to list himself in local directories as a "Landscape Painter." In 1832 he settled in Boston for five prosperous years—and then, in his new-found affluence, he set off for England where he studied for two years. On his return he bought a house in Newburgh, New York, and joined the Hudson River painters.

His paintings received favorable critical attention, his work was engraved and lithographed in many publications, and the Art Union paid five hundred dollars apiece for his landscapes. But within a few years the public was seeking more inspiration and less formula. The Art Union stopped buying Doughty's works, and though history now acknowledges Doughty as the first successful American landscape painter and the first to express the

"In the Catskills" by Thomas Doughty. ADDISON GALLERY OF ART, PHILLIPS ACADEMY, ANDOVER

poetry of America's nature, he died in relative poverty and obscurity.

The painters of the Hudson River School had more in common than the geographical area in which they worked. An analysis of Doughty's work tells much about the entire school and the traits that were typical not only of the school, but of American sensibility.

This was the same period in which the members of the Barbizon school of painters—Millet, Corot, and Rousseau—were active in France. They, too, were interested in landscape. But unlike Doughty who took a panoramic view of nature, encompassing miles of space in his compositions, the Barbizon painters portrayed limited views, focusing on atmospheric details and intimate pictorial subjects. While Millet might concentrate on a small glen, a stream, a house, and a few head of cattle, Doughty sought to record nature in all its vastness and complexity, from foreground to far-off horizon. Much like wide-lens, panoramic photographs, his paintings were infinitely detailed. They included minute renderings of each tree, leaf, blade of grass, flower, cloud, mountain, man, and wild creature.

Line was the essence, the very spirit and basis of his work. Color was secondary to drawing, giving Doughty's work, and that of all the Hudson River artists, a precision, clarity, sharpness of contour, and bold delineation of shapes that make American landscapes distinctive and easily recognizable in contrast with the work of European painters, who were more concerned with plasticity and lively brushwork than with linear definition. Looking back to the beginnings of American art, we can discover the roots of this linear definition in Puritan portraits and the earliest American paintings of scenes and people.

A very minor nonconformist, Doughty relieved the over-all monotony of his technique by allowing brushstrokes to remain undisturbed on the canvas instead of fusing them together in the hard and porcelain-like finish so beloved of the neoclassicists. This textural effect gave his paintings some liveliness and vitality, but it never adequately compensated for his emphasis on unimportant details.

At best, Doughty was just another popular artist who painted upstate New York and the Catskills during the first half of the nineteenth century. But he did focus on landscape, inspiring and encouraging other, more imaginative artists to do the same, suggesting the infinite possibilities of subject and theme that could be found beyond the cities in the wilderness hitherto undiscovered by the white man. More than his painting, this inspiration was Thomas Doughty's contribution to American art.

On a November day in 1825 as New York City was celebrating the opening of the Erie Canal, John Trumbull walked past the shop of a frame maker who had just placed in his window three paintings by an unknown young artist. For the famed old American painter this was a profound moment of discovery—there, in the window of this small commercial shop, Trumbull saw three amazing depictions of his beloved native land, executed with magnificent skill and remarkable realism, yet not without the gentle warmth of the poet.

Almost unable to believe his eyes, he rushed off to the studio of his friend, William Dunlap, another veteran painter of the Revolutionary years. "This young man," he exclaimed, "has done what all my life I attempted in vain to do!"

Dunlap returned with Trumbull to the frame shop, and the young artist, twenty-four-year-old Thomas Cole, was summoned to meet the great men. "When I saw the pictures," Dunlap wrote at a later date, "I found them to exceed all that this praise had led me to expect. . . . Cole stood like a schoolboy in the presence of the trustees, neither of whom could produce a rival to the works he was offering for the paltry price of twenty-five dollars each."

Shy, pale, overawed in the presence of New York's best-known painter, the man who had created the four major murals in the rotunda of the Capitol in Washington, D.C., and another almost equally famed artist, Cole stammered and stuttered as he answered questions about his background and training. "You surprise me!" Trumbull repeated over and over. "You surprise me!"

And indeed he might, for Thomas Cole's was a surprising story.

The first American artist to portray nature effectively in personal, imaginative, inventive, and romantic terms, Thomas Cole was born in England in 1801 and did not come to America until he was seventeen. He stayed for a while in Philadelphia to work as a wood engraver and then followed his family to Steubenville, Ohio, by walking three hundred miles across the mountains. Walking, he felt, was always a most important part of his art. Later in life he wrote, "To walk with nature as a poet is the necessary condition of the perfect artist."

An itinerant peddler from Virginia named Stein was the man who changed Cole's world. Stein not only sold an odd assortment of wonderful wares, but he carried with him paints and empty oblongs of canvas. As young Cole watched, openmouthed with wonder, Stein brought to life the shapes, forms and personalities of people with brush and color. The peddler gave the boy a book. "It was an English work on painting," Cole wrote, "illustrated with engravings and treated of design, composition, color. This book was my constant companion, night and day. . . . My ambition grew and in my imagination I pictured the glories of being a great painter."

With no further instruction, but with a pack filled with canvases, raw paints, oil, brushes, and a heavy stone muller strapped to his back, and the saddle he had received as payment for his very first portrait—which would have been very useful if he'd had a horse—Cole started walking through the woods of Ohio, on into Pennsylvania and New York, seeking portrait commissions in exchange for food, lodging, and whatever else he might get in payment. Along the way he stopped to study for a short time at the Pennsylvania Academy of Fine Arts, and there he was impressed and inspired by the work of Thomas Doughty. Then off he went again, with his pack on his back, up and down the Hudson Valley, across the Adirondacks and the Catskills, the White and the Green Mountains—discovering that he would rather paint landscapes than people; recording ideas, drawings, color notes, and emotional reactions in a pad that was as much diary as sketchbook. "How I have walked!" he exclaimed to a friend. "Day after day, and all alone."

"The Oxbow (The Connecticut River near Northampton)" by Thomas Cole. THE METROPOLITAN MUSEUM OF ART, GIFT OF MRS. RUSSELL SAGE, 1908

During the summer of 1825, hiking along the valley of the Hudson on the approach to the Catskills, he was overwhelmed by the breadth and movement of the river, the untamed forests, the quiet strips of cultivated fields, and the mountains in the distance, "covered with glorious trees, ever changing in color, light and shadow." Years later, after Cole had seen the Rhine, he was to write that "in natural magnificence and grandeur . . . it was infinitely inferior to the Hudson."

Carrying his sketches of the river and the mountains back to New York, he found an attic room where, "perpetually fighting with a kind of twilight . . . elbowed and pushed by mean partitions," he transferred his ideas, sketches, and emotions onto canvas. According to art historian James Thomas Flexner, "To the old pallid shapes he brought violence of handling; leaves brushed in as by a giant, rocks ponderous, shaggy mountains swelling irresistibly from the pitching lowlands. His color was both strong and tender; greens virginal or hoary, shading to gold in the sunlight; lakes agleam; skies sometimes gentle, sometimes blackly vaporous. Here was exuberance and power, a conviction of importance, an expression of beauty that had never before been brought to renditions of the American land."

These were the pictures Trumbull had seen in the frame shop, offered for sale at twenty-five dollars apiece.

Cole's view was everything Flexner says it was—and it was patriotic as well. "American scenes," Cole wrote, "are not destitute of historical and legendary associations; the great struggle for freedom has sanctified many a spot, and many a mountain stream and rock has its legend, worthy of a poet's pen or painter's pencil . . . where the wolf roams the plow shall glisten; on the grey crag shall rise temple and tower . . . the painter of American scenery has indeed privileges superior to any other. All nature here is new to art."

Unlike Doughty, whose paintings all had a detailed realistic sameness, Cole emphasized subject, feeling that it contributed mood, established the emotional attitudes of the painting as well as the artist, and stimulated the imagination of artist and viewer alike. "If the imagination is shackled," he wrote, "seldom will anything great be produced in painting or in poetry."

He gloried in light and dark patterns, called chiaroscuro, that shifted and played against each other with dramatic contrast. His lights were very light, and his darks ranged from merely deep to lamp black. "Light is the great stimulant," he wrote. "It is the fire of life."

His use of chiaroscuro can be seen in the "Expulsion from the Garden of Eden," painted in 1828 when his constantly increasing interest in religion began to be expressed in his work. No longer was he looking at nature alone. He was looking inward into his own soul and making discoveries that would eventually send him searching in many directions and create a confusion in his mind and a confused variety in his work.

In his notebook, close to the sketches he used when painting the "Expulsion," he wrote: "Alone as I was on the shore of that dark, unrippled water, with towering precipices above . . .

"Expulsion from the Garden of Eden" by Thomas Cole. COURTESY,
MUSEUM OF FINE ARTS, BOSTON. KAROLIK COLLECTION

where the voice of man was not heard nor the sound of the ax,
there was an awfulness in the utter solitude that was almost painful. Many may seek such scenes and find pleasure in the discovery,
but there is a mysterious fear comes over him and hurries him
away. The sublime features of nature are too severe for a lone
man to look upon and be happy."

Although Cole had borrowed the design for the "Expulsion"
from a print by the English artist John Martin, he gave it grandeur, drama, theatricality, and power that were nowhere to be
found in the original. The lush, green Garden of Eden stands in
sharp, bright contrast to the dark, barren, eerie dead quality of
the world outside. Across a rocky bridge joining the two oppo-
sites of the composition pass the minute, almost indistinguishable
forms of Adam and Eve. The figures, driven out of Eden, have
passed into darkness through an opening in the huge rock bar-

rier through which intense beams of brilliant light are bursting. The heavens swirl—twisted with light and dark patterns of clouds, almost as operatic background music, charging the biblical scene with intense emotionality. Cecil B. De Mille, famed maker of highly charged pseudobiblical and historical motion pictures, could very well have taken ideas and inspiration from this painting.

Cole dramatized the scene with landscape elements sketched on his walking tours—a chasm and churning waterfalls; twisted, tortured trees; driving storms splitting the heavens; idyllic glens. The same elements combined in another context without the religious intensity could have produced any of his warm and peaceful paeans to the American wilderness.

The figures in the "Expulsion," as in most of Cole's works, are small and play a relatively minor role. Cole was not a skillful figure painter, and he avoided painting figures when he could, preferring to see man and his works as a small and rather impermanent aspect in the great scheme of nature.

Possibly at the height of his career, Cole left for the grand tour of Europe. Fearing that Cole, like John Singleton Copley, might lose much of his untutored American power in exchange for sophisticated European tricks, his friend, the poet William Cullen Bryant wrote:

To Cole, The Painter, Departing For Europe

Thine eyes shall see the light of distant skies:
Yet, Cole! thy heart shall bear to Europe's strand
A living image of our own bright land,
Such as upon thy glorious canvas lies.
Lone lakes—savannahs where the bison roves—
Skies where the desert eagle wheels and screams—
Spring bloom and autumn blaze of boundless groves.

Fair scenes shall greet thee where thou goest—fair
But different—everywhere the trace of men.
Paths, homes, graves, ruins, from the lowest glen

To where life shrinks from the fierce alpine air.
Gaze on them, till the tears shall dim thy sight
But keep that earlier, wilder image bright.

His words were prophetic. Though Cole returned in 1832 with his patriotic and religious sentiments strengthened and settled down in the village of Catskill in his beloved wild Hudson Valley, he began to paint huge, neoclassic allegories of minor interest, illustrating the "Course of Empire" and "The Voyage of Life"— cosmic dramas, but hardly profound or original ones.

"There were really two Thomas Coles," art historian Oliver W. Larkin wrote. "One pictured the 'Oxbow' very much as it looked, knowing that the 'dollar-godded' patron preferred it so. The other succumbed . . . to 'the poetry of decay,' in Europe. . . . A few artists and laymen, even while Cole lived preferred his topography to his theology . . . suggesting that the darkness of allegory was vanishing before common sense."

Just before his untimely death in 1848, Cole may have been making the same discovery for himself. His romance with the American wilderness burst forth anew, and he sailed for Mount Desert Island off the coast of Maine, and almost as if he knew this was his last affair with his true love, landscape, he made some of the best drawings of his career.

"Go first to nature and learn to paint landscape," Asher Brown Durand urged his students at the National Academy. When they could imitate scrupulously whatever she presents, then and only then could they study with profit the paintings of the great masters. "And walk," he advised. A painter should spend every summer walking under the sky, keeping his eye keen, seeking always new beauties and new vistas.

Asher Brown Durand, a New Jersey-born engraver who was past the age of forty when he commenced painting, was the first of Cole's disciples, in terms of time as well as quality. When he first met Cole, Durand was already renowned and successful in his own field, especially for his reproductions of Trumbull's "Declaration of Independence," a three-year, fine-line labor on copper completed when he was twenty-seven, and John Vanderlyn's "Ariadne."

A religious man with deeply ingrained Puritanism, Durand avoided all traditional institutions, especially churches, in his search for inspiration. Instead, he celebrated the Sabbath by walking in the woods. "Nature," he wrote, ". . . is fraught with high and holy meaning, only surpassed by the light of Revelation." He believed that an artist who painted a landscape faithful to God's divine work was creating a visual sermon that would elevate all who viewed it. It was this belief that led to the sensational popularity of the Hudson River painters.

Finally, here was an argument for art that fitted the nation's Puritan traditions while vanquishing the democratic ethic that art was a useless luxury in a practical society. The moral, the practical, and the pragmatic all could be satisfied simultaneously, for pictures of untrammeled nature brought God's word to the people. As a result landscapes over American fireplaces became as common as Bibles on living room tables.

To those who argued that nationalism limited the universality of art, Durand pointed out that scenery spared from the pollution of civilization guaranteed originality and that, therefore, Americans could originate a high and independent style based on their own resources in accordance with principles of self-government. "Go not abroad," he advised his students, "in search of material for the exercise of your pencil while the virgin charms of our own native land have claims on our deepest affections." In 1840, putting aside his own advice, he took three students to Europe for a year, seeing and absorbing all he could in the art capitals of the Old World, but ending up "bewildered, wretched and homesick."

The meticulousness and attention to detail that were so evident in his engraving became the hallmark of his painting. "I paint green," he said, "because I see nature as green." Other colors in nature he saw as tints, and he held all color in place with what had been his basic tool in engraving, values of black and white.

Gray was most important to a landscape painter, he claimed, since it allowed variations within local color without weakening it. Durand worked more in terms of light and dark, keeping his use of color to a minimum. As a result, although his work shows up very well in black and white illustrations, a harshness marks its true color.

One of his most characteristic works, except for the size of the figures, is "Kindred Spirits," painted in 1849, in which his frock-coated friends, William Cullen Bryant and Thomas Cole, stand on a mountain ledge framed against a spacious and idyllic Catskill Mountain gorge. Bryant had delivered the eulogy at Cole's funeral, and Durand painted this picture as a gift to the poet to record his own friendship for the two men and the close, intimate feelings they all shared for nature. Despite the emotion that motivated him, the painting is true to Durand's lifelong style—filled with details and accuracy rather than sentiment.

After Cole's death Durand became the acknowledged leader of the Hudson River School. He was president of the National Academy from 1846 to 1861 and, as a result, had great impact on a generation of younger artists and on the landscape painting that followed in the young, exuberant, and expanding nation.

John Frederick Kensett was one of the most popular, and evidently one of the most financially successful, of the Hudson River painters—at his death in 1872 a public auction of the contents of his studio brought $137,715. Like Durand, he had been an engraver before he became a painter, and he was one of the students who accompanied Durand to Europe. But when the others returned, he stayed on for seven additional years. Showing more interest in seeing the landscape than in painting it, he took very much to heart Cole's dictum to "walk with nature as a poet."

Shoe leather took him from one end of the British Isles to the other, through the forests of Fontainebleau, across the Rhine, over the Alps, down to Venice and Florence and Rome. Back in America he retraced Cole's steps and went beyond them—all the time recording what he saw in thin, sharp, competent sketches.

When he finally settled into a studio, he turned out innumerable well-structured and orderly compositions. He retained all the precise detail of the earlier Hudson River men, maintaining sharp definition and unwavering focus on the elements of nature. He was the most subtle colorist of the group, usually constructing his thinly-smooth compositions in broad areas of sky, sea, and land. His best works have a delicate poetry and slightly melancholy mood. More than any of the others he was concerned with the hushed moment in time—a theme that was soon to be explored much more intensely by the Frenchman Claude Monet and which would launch the Impressionist School.

A contemporary critic summed up Kensett as: "The Bryant of our painters, a little sad and monotonous, but sweet, artistic and unaffected."

America's taste in art had gravitated away from the cold classical clarity of John Trumbull's work. Shortly before the Civil War began several artists received commissions from Congress for paintings to complete the decoration of the Capitol in Washington, D.C., and by then the demand was for dramatic, stirring, emotional scenes.

Curiously, most of the artists sought the inspiration of Europe for their "typical American scenes," following in the steps of Horatio Greenough, sculptor of the famed Washington. For "Baptism of Pocahontas," commissioned for the rotunda, John Gadsby Chapman went not to Virginia, but to Rome.

To paint "The Discovery of the Mississippi," also for the rotunda, Walter Weir sought his inspiration on the banks of the Seine in Paris. The color, clash, and bombast of these and other paintings that filled the Capitol gained more distinction as theatrical masquerades than as art.

The most renowned of these pseudo-American historical potboilers was painted by Emanuel Leutze who lived and worked in Düsseldorf, then the art training center of Germany. As one of Germany's most famed teachers, his historical paintings were greatly admired in America. After only three years of study in this country Leutze was considered enough of an American artist to warrant the Capitol commission. He promptly returned to Germany, and there beside the Rhine River he painted "Washington Crossing the Delaware," which was later reproduced in countless history books and stirred the patriotic emotions of Americans for decades to come. Although he continued living in Germany, Leutze became a permanent figure in the annals of American painting.

When Leutze's painting was exhibited in the Capitol in 1852, Congress was so impressed they immediately commissioned him to portray "Westward the Course of Empire Takes Its Way" for the west stairway of the House wing. This painting dealt with the crossing of the Rocky Mountains. Instead of going to the Alps for his research, Leutze went to the Rockies, but the result of his on-the-spot studies was anything but successful.

"Westward the Course of Empire," which is not an oil painting but a stereochromy watercolor applied directly to plaster, is a huge, overdone, theatrical cornball, filled with unimportant details and sweeping patterns of dark and light that fail to hold the composition together in any sort of unified mass.

A contemporary critic summed it all up quite succinctly, "Düsseldorf schmaltz!"—doing more for the American language in one second than Leutze did for American art in his lifetime.

[7]

DECADES OF THE UNCOMMON MAN

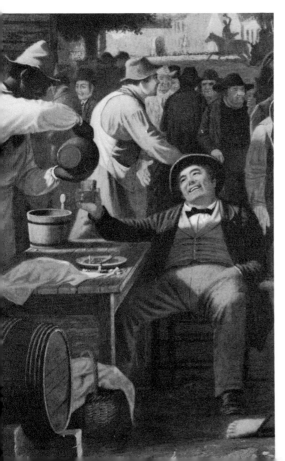

Detail from "The County Election" by George Caleb Bingham. CITY ART MUSEUM OF SAINT LOUIS

J ohn James Audubon was a man of stature, talent, and, most overwhelmingly, imagination. Numerous biographies have been written about him, including several that attempt to prove him the "lost Dauphin" of France—a surmise that he rather enjoyed and encouraged. He was, in fact, the illegitimate son of a French sea captain and a Santo Domingo Creole.

An unsuccessful American backwoods storekeeper, a bankrupt jailbird, an adventurer, a buckskinned social success in sophisticated London—Audubon was also the greatest painter of wildlife that America, and possibly the entire world, had ever known. He was born in Haiti in 1785. Several years later his father took him to France for his education where it is believed he studied drawing with the great French master David. In 1804 his father sent him to look after some properties he owned in America. Just how scrupulously he fulfilled this assignment is open to speculation, but we do know that he wooed and won the hand of sixteen-year-old Lucy

Bakewell. The couple took off via coach and flatboat for Louisville, Kentucky, where Audubon opened a general store. Business was not all that good so he spent a large part of his time hunting. Birds were his primary targets, for they not only provided dinner for his family but served as models for his paintings. His interest in wildlife—which had begun when he lived with his father's family in Nantes, France—soon overcame his ambition for business.

He solved that immediate problem by moving Lucy and their infant son 125 miles farther down the Ohio River by skiff to a village called Henderson, where he set up a new store. There he found less business and more birds. Eventually the store failed, and Audubon was sent to jail as a debtor while Lucy found a job as a governess.

As soon as he was released from jail, the Audubons went to Louisiana. Lucy took a job teaching school to support the family, and John James, whose interest in birds was now an intense personal passion, decided on a career as an artist. "If I were jealous," Lucy is reported to have said, "I should have a bitter time of it, for every bird is my rival." He riveted his attention on wildlife and portrayed it with remarkable accuracy. His spirit and soul, his whole being was drawn to birds, and his eyes and mind studied them in their natural habitat while his unerring hand recorded their features, form, and action with incredible speed. A note attached to a drawing of a rooster and hens reads: "These chickens were painted by John James Audubon in one morning before one o'clock lunch, as someone visiting him told him he did not believe such rapid work could be done."

In 1824, loaded down with hundreds of pictures and determined to have them published in a book, he left his family and went to Philadelphia, then the nation's center of science and publishing. Tall, muscular, long-haired, dressed in the fringed buckskins of the frontier, with dagger and tomahawk at his waist and leather moccasins on his feet, he was scorned as an illiterate savage by the proper Philadelphians: How could the work of such a backwoodsman be of any cultural value?

The reaction in New York was no better. In his passionate search for acceptance he boarded a ship for England in 1826 with his portfolio of watercolor drawings and letters of introduction from the Philadelphia portraitist Sully as his only capital. The very characteristics that were looked down on in Philadelphia made him a social lion in London. The English looked on him as a colorful character and invited him into their drawing rooms to hear his imitations of bird calls. His long hair, he wrote to Lucy, "does as much for me as my talent for painting."

One critic wrote: "Brave is the exhibition of flowing locks; they flow over the ears and over the coat collar; you can smell the bear's grease across the street."

Queried about encounters with wild animals, Audubon admitted, "I've never been troubled by any animals larger than ticks."

Another London journalist wrote: "The tall and somewhat stooping form, the clothes made not by a West End but by a Far West tailor, the steady, rapid, springing step, the long hair, the aquiline features, and the glowing, angry eyes—the expression of a handsome man conscious of ceasing to be young, and an air and manner which told you that whatever you might be he was John Audubon, will never be forgotten by anyone who knew or saw him."

The events of the ten years that followed make one of the most fantastic stories of talent and energy in the history of American art. He succeeded in having his drawings published—he found engravers to produce the plates, sold subscriptions, acted as his own publisher, painted replicas of his originals to sell for living expenses, wrote the scientific information and charming, lively essays that lightened the text, traveled back and forth to America to complete the series of birds, oversaw the engraving, colored the first plates and finally brought out four double-elephant folio volumes of *The Birds of America, from Original Drawings, with 435 Plates Showing 1,065 Figures.*

The Birds of America appeared between 1827 and 1838, and the accompanying text, five volumes of the *Ornithological Bi-*

ography, between 1831 and 1839. The combined effort of writing and painting make this a monumental work, one of the great scientific and artistic achievements of the nineteenth century.

Returning to America, he offered to share his financial triumph with Lucy who had been on her own for twenty years. Believing that she might help to keep him organized and out of financial difficulties, Lucy agreed, and they bought an estate in New York on the Hudson River. Between traveling and painting he helped his good friend Samuel Morse tinker with early models of the gadget that later became the telegraph and taught his painting methods to his sons, John and Victor.

With his sons as assistants he launched into his last major work, a series of 150 paintings of animals, published in 1845 as *The Viviparous Quadrupeds of North America*. But the paintings were largely the work of his sons and in no way equal to Audubon's birds.

Some scientists belittle Audubon's accomplishment, claiming that he discovered no new species, had little interest in classification, and that at times he painted birds in positions the birds could not possibly have assumed. They say, too, that he displayed an excess of emotion that sometimes interfered with accurate rendering. A great scientist, they argued, would have treated his subject more dispassionately and would have made his artistic accomplishments secondary to scientific accuracy.

But John James Audubon was primarily an artist—and a superb one. His line was precise and splendid, with clarity, grace, and total refinement of forms. His colors were as fresh, vital, and lively as possible, considering the limitations and tricky quality of fast-drying watercolor, and his work in oil retained the same brilliance and freshness.

Audubon's theme was nature—and in his small subjects he showed it with all of its wild, colorful, and complex splendor. He sought to depict birds factually, honestly, and accurately, and here he succeeded, with his love and enthusiasm for wildlife bringing to his work a never-surpassed vitality, beauty, and drama.

Of all the artists who followed the migrations westward—in the van of the trappers, the rivermen, the traders, and the cowboys—of all the painters who portrayed the last rugged and provincial outposts of the white man, George Caleb Bingham was the greatest. Working out of St. Louis, far from the schools and galleries of the sophisticated East, he became the first great painter of the Midwest—and one of the most original and competent painters in America.

Bingham was born in Virginia, and at the age of eight he migrated with his family to Missouri. About a year later he was introduced to Chester Harding, an artist traveling through Missouri on the trail of a portrait of Daniel Boone. Harding stimulated the lad's interest in art. With some homemade pigments and brushes, whatever other materials he could find in frontier stores, and copies of European engravings his schoolteacher mother had brought from Virginia, Bingham started to paint.

For a while he earned a living rolling cigars. At sixteen he was apprenticed to a cabinetmaker for whom he was soon painting signs. A second visit from Harding taught him enough about painting to send him up and down the river at twenty-two as an itinerant portraitist. At twenty-six he left Missouri for a few months to study at the Pennsylvania Academy of Fine Arts in Philadelphia where he made the most of observing the paintings of American masters—West, Allston, Sully, and Lawrence—as well as the work of some of the great Europeans.

He went back to Missouri when his money ran out. Thrilled with the improvements that had resulted from his few months of training and his astonishing capacity to absorb a knowledge of drawing and composition by simple study, he began painting banners and delivering speeches in William Henry Harrison's presidential campaign. Following the victor to Washington, he set up a studio in a shanty at the foot of Capitol Hill and waited for famous subjects to find him, but few made the effort. John Quincy Adams did, and he regretted it, refusing to accept his portrait when it was completed.

The presidential election of 1844 brought him back to Missouri for more speeches and bigger banners. But Clay was defeated by Polk, and not wishing to return to the capital while it was presided over by his political opponents, Bingham remained in Missouri and found himself catapulted into his true greatness.

Six years earlier, in New York, he had sold a river scene to the Apollo Gallery—and had been told that easterners were curious about everyday aspects of Western life. Seeking recognition in New York, and certain that he wouldn't achieve it on the basis of portraits of Missourians, he began painting genre scenes of life along the river. The directors of the American Art Union which had succeeded the Apollo Gallery bought everything he offered, wrote critical raves in their publications, distributed engravings by the thousands—and suddenly George Caleb Bingham was famous.

He painted innumerable views of life along the Mississippi and Missouri rivers, but he never showed anyone at work or raising a sweat through any activity more strenuous than dancing, drink-

"The County Election" by George Caleb Bingham. CITY ART MUSEUM OF SAINT LOUIS

ing, or politicking. He portrayed fur traders drifting downriver, raftsmen playing cards, racing steamboats, shooting matches, farmers, checkers games. His scenes of political campaigns and elections provide a vivid pictorial history of frontier democracy, of the life and attitudes of wilderness-edge communities. Always a political activist, he was far from the dispassionate observer. His paintings satirized opponents as huge and bestial brutes and delineated his favored candidates as young, earnest, and attractive.

Through the distribution of engravings he became the East's favorite illustrator of the frontier. But he was far more than a social illustrator—he was a serious and talented fine artist. And nowhere are his talent, depth, and subtlety more evident than in his masterful canvas "Fur Traders Descending the Missouri."

"Fur Traders Descending the Missouri" is a superb example of George Caleb Bingham's craftsmanship and sensitive color harmonies. THE METROPOLITAN MUSEUM OF ART, MORRIS K. JESUP FUND, 1933

Here a poetic quality, imagination, draftsmanship, and sensitive color harmonies combine to create a suspenseful mood of mystery and solitude that go far beyond mere illustration. A brilliant luminosity, a wealth of color tones despite an over-all haze of sunlight, subtle gradations of light and color, airiness and spaciousness, grandeur and solemnity all combine to give his frontiersmen the heroic flavor of immortality. It is truly amazing how Bingham, with only the most cursory and rudimentary exposure to the great art of the past, was able to absorb so many of its lessons.

In 1856 he went to Düsseldorf to study. There his work acquired a certain German schmaltz and sentimentality. When he returned to the United States in 1859, the Civil War was brewing and frontier politics were boiling over. Favoring the Union in the Civil War, Bingham put aside his palette for politics and became Missouri's state treasurer from 1862 to 1865. The stronger he became in politics, the weaker he grew at his painting, until eventually he surrendered completely and put away his brushes forever. In 1875 he became the state's adjutant general, and at his death in 1879 he was eulogized as a statesman, his ability as an artist all but forgotten.

It took time and history to put things back into their proper perspective, and today Bingham is recognized as one of America's truly great painters and as an integral part of the land he painted.

Just as Bingham was the greatest of the painters who followed the white man to civilization's edge, George Catlin was the most remarkable of those who went beyond that edge into the limitless areas of the Great Plains—the land of the Indian and the buffalo. Between 1830 and 1836 he visited, lived with, and painted the Indian tribes scattered over the little-known area of the upper Missouri, and from the headwaters of the Mississippi to the deserts of the great Southwest.

He made the most comprehensive pictorial record that exists of these Indians in their normal environment, rendering scores of portraits of chiefs, warriors, medicine men, braves, women, and children; scenes of tribal ceremonials, dances, games, warfare, hunting, burial, and other activities. He also wrote a detailed and eloquent record to supplement his pictures. His books were strong emotional appeals to halt the attacks of civilization on his helpless red friends. In his years of travel he visited forty-eight tribes and completed more than six hundred paintings. He brought back wagonloads of decorated skin garments, ceremonial paraphernalia, weapons, artifacts, utensils, and finery. He made an invaluable contribution not only to American art but also to anthropology.

Although the Indian didn't know it, Catlin sensed that Indian culture—at the end of the golden age that had begun with the introduction of the horse into the New World by the Spanish conquistadores—was poised on the brink of destruction. The Indian was free, prosperous, happy, generous, friendly, and valiant. The early rivalry between white man and red had abated. The Mississippi Valley was settled and reasonably peaceful, and the white man was filling the area eastward to the Alleghenies. West of the Mississippi—in the plains, the badlands, the mountains, and the desert—the Indian still ruled, stalking the buffalo, lassoing his wild horses, brandishing his feathered war lance, making hallowed the hunting and burial grounds of his ancestors. Gold had not yet been discovered in California, nor was the East yet overcrowded, nor the wagons rolling westward. And since the white man did not yet want what the Indian had, the Indian could continue to live as his forefathers had.

Until Catlin painted the area, it was unknown to all men except the aborigines and a few intrepid fur traders and explorers. To most Americans the Indian was an exotic, untamed creature presented in paintings either as a grotesque European in feathers performing barbaric rituals or as a high-minded philosophical savage.

As the country expanded westward, the general attitude toward the Indians shifted from curiosity to hostility, and Indians were soon considered wasteful, hostile occupants of millions of acres of valuable agricultural, pasture, and mineral lands. The fact that it was *their* land was ignored. Puritan tradition was on the side of the white man. The Indians were heathens who failed to follow God's command to "Occupy the earth, increase and multiply."

The whole history of the winning of the West has been written from the white man's viewpoint, and thus Catlin's remarks, written 130 years ago, were extremely unpopular—despite their truth and Catlin's eloquent conviction.

"I love a people," Catlin wrote, "who have always made me welcome . . . who are honest without laws, who have no jails and no poor house . . . who never take the name of God in vain . . . who worship God without a bible, and I believe that God loves them also . . . who are free from religious animosities . . . who never raised a hand against me, or have stolen my property . . . who never fought a battle with white men except on their own ground . . . and how I love a people who don't live for the love of money."

Fearing that the beauty of the untamed tribes would vanish with the onrush of the white man, he pleaded for a park, comprising most of the plains country, to be set aside by the government, where the free-roving Indian could live undisturbed to inspire future ages. They are "knights of the forest," he wrote, "whose lives are lives of chivalry and whose daily feats, with their naked limbs, must vie with the Grecian youths in the beautiful rivalry of the Olympic games."

Much later, after his message had been long unheeded and the Indians were being driven from their lands and slaughtered, in tortured anguish, Catlin wrote, "I have seen the grand and irresistible march of civilization . . . this splendid juggernaut rolling on and beheld its sweeping desolation."

Catlin's opinions have been sources of bitter controversy for generations. Taught to believe that Indians were either subhuman or part god, the American public refused to believe his factual paintings or reports.

As for his art, that, too, has been as controversial as the Indians he drew with his quick and sympathetic brush. His paintings have been both praised and condemned. To some Catlin was a

Romanticist, to others a Realist, still others consider him an American Primitive. Much of this confusion resulted from the inability of certain critics and teachers, as well as part of the public, to realize that documentary painting is a viable and worthy art in itself. Truthful, accurate, lively, animated, forceful, colorful, Catlin's paintings possess deep artistic qualities. His feelings, emotions, and attitudes gave his work the personal and distinctive quality essential to all great works of art—they are an individual comment, deserving more respect than history and his contemporaries gave him.

A thin, wiry, leather-tough man, about five feet, eight inches tall, weighing about 135 pounds, George Catlin had the dark complexion, hooknosed face, and black hair of an Indian. Only his bright blue eyes set him apart from the aborigines he painted. Modest and charitable, he was a warm and friendly man, with a deep sense of morality and religion. His interest in the red man had been piqued at an early age by tales of the wilderness and Indian atrocities told by survivors of the bloodiest Indian raids of the American Revolution, in the Wyoming Valley of Pennsylvania where he was reared. Playacting as an Indian at the age of ten, a friend threw a tomahawk that glanced off a tree and gashed a wound that left a long scar on Catlin's cheek.

His father, a successful lawyer, sent him to law school, but the youth, scorning book learning, decided to become an artist, and determinedly set about teaching himself the theory and technique of painting. His boyhood fascination with Indians was rekindled by the sight of a delegation of chiefs from the Far West parading through Philadelphia on the way to Washington. This group, "arranged in all their classic beauty, with shield and helmet—with tunic and manteau—tinted and tasselled off, exactly for the painter's palette . . ." made a deep impression, and he resolved that "the history and customs of such a people, preserved by pictorial illustrations, are themes worthy of the lifetime of one man, and nothing short of the loss of my life shall prevent me from visiting their country, and becoming their historian."

Although he was enjoying reasonable success as a portrait

painter, he began making trips to the Indian reservations in western New York, painting portraits of the Iroquois and Seneca chiefs and whetting his appetite to visit the Far West to bring home "faithful portraits of their principal personages . . . and snatch from hasty oblivion . . . a truly lofty and noble race."

St. Louis was the gateway to the Western wilderness. It was headquarters for the fur companies, both large and small, and for the trappers, hunters, wilderness men, and adventurers who were trading with the Indians and opening up the frontiers. It was a booming, bustling, roaring frontier town, official head-quarters for the Army of the West and Northwest, ruled over by the military governor, General William Clark (of the Lewis and Clark Expedition of 1805), who was also superintendent of In-dian Affairs. Catlin journeyed to St. Louis, showed his portraits of the New York State Indians to General Clark, and enlisted his aid in his project.

Clark not only allowed Catlin to paint portraits of many of the chiefs who visited his office, but he sat for his own portrait and al-lowed Catlin to accompany him on field trips to Indian villages for ceremonials, treaties, and powwows.

When the American Fur Company, owned by John Jacob Astor, sent its first steamboat up the Missouri River, Catlin was aboard. He sailed two thousand miles upriver into an almost completely uncivilized country, into the primitive, warlike world of the Crows and the Blackfeet, ending up at Fort Union in what is now northwest South Dakota. When the steamboat returned, Catlin stayed behind at the fort, to make his way back to St. Louis alone by canoe, stopping along the way to paint his Indian friends in their primitive riverbank villages.

In 1834 he started out from Fort Gibson and crossed the South-western plains to the Rockies, remaining during a siege of illness with the Comanches. In 1835 he sailed up the Mississippi to its source and then up the Des Moines River to live with the Sioux and the Foxes—and wherever he went he carried a tin case of rolled up canvases, pigments, oil, and brushes.

He traveled alone, by canoe, dugout, horseback, and on foot, in a land where "The buffaloes range with the elk and the fleet bounding antelope; where wolves are white and bears are grizzly; where rivers are yellow . . . the dogs are all wolves, women are slaves, men all lords . . . where the predominant passions of the savage breast are ferocity and honor." He was well received by friendly, hospitable people who he found had "feelings to meet feelings." He made friends quickly and chiefs posed patiently for portraits. He was allowed to witness and even to participate in their most secret and sacred religious rituals.

His method of painting was strongly influenced by his need for speed. Many of the Indians grew impatient sitting, but Catlin's sharp and retentive memory enabled him to complete the paintings at a later time. Many were completed in the office of General Clark in St. Louis, with whom he had maintained a close friendship.

Just how fast he worked is illustrated by the fact that during an 86-day period in 1832, he produced 135 pictures, including 66 portraits, 25 landscapes, and 44 genre scenes, all while traveling fifteen hundred miles, taking part in Indian ceremonies, holding long and tedious powwows with Indians and fur traders, hunting for food, and being incapacitated by illness.

Persuading the chiefs to sit was not always an easy task. Never having seen a likeness on canvas before, many of the Indians were stunned and frightened by the idea. The renowned chief of the Sioux, The One Horn—a mighty warrior, reputed to be able to run down a buffalo on his own legs and drive an arrow into its heart—posed for Catlin in a wigwam decorated with the scalps of his enemies, and then made Catlin hang the painting outside where all could admire it and be impressed by The One Horn's courage. The other chiefs were so pleased they conferred on Catlin the title of "Medicine Painter," elevating him to the status of medicine man.

But even then, different crafts had proud little cliques, and rather than accept the white man, jealous medicine men stirred up trouble by spreading the tale that because the eyes on the painting were always open, the painted chief would never be able to sleep again. They predicted bad luck and an early death. As the braves and women of the village milled around, The One Horn came to Catlin's rescue by praising the painter and denying he was unable to sleep. Once logic overcame terror and superstition, the rest of the chiefs took their places in line, eagerly waiting their turns to sit for portraits in Catlin's wigwam studio.

When Catlin returned to the East, he organized an exhibit, modeled after Peale's museum, of his Indian paintings. Failing to gain recognition in the United States for either his work or his ideas, Catlin took his Indian Gallery to Europe in 1839. For many years he roamed England and the continent with a combined art show-museum-wild west show, even bringing several braves to London to enact a war dance. In 1846, by command of King Louis Philippe, his entire gallery was exhibited in the Louvre and two of his Indian portraits were included in the Salon Show of Paris that year.

Catlin wrote in his exhibition catalogue that ". . . every painting has been made from nature by my own hand—and that too when I have been paddling my canoe or leading my pack horse over and through trackless wilds, at the hazard of my life—the world will surely be kind and indulgent enough to receive and estimate them . . . as true and facsimile traces of individual life and historical fact, and forgive me their present unfinished and unstudied condition as works of art."

In reviewing the Salon Show, Baudelaire did more than forgive him. He wrote, "The rumor went out that he is a worthy man who could neither paint nor draw. . . . It is demonstrated today that Mr. Catlin knows very well how to paint and draw. These two portraits would suffice to prove it to me, if my memory did not bring back many other pieces equally fine."

But in spite of this, the going was long, slow, and rough, and once the novelty of his show wore off, Catlin failed. In 1851 he was out of business. The next year Daniel Webster, addressing the Senate, pleaded in vain that the collection be purchased as a national treasure. "The Indian likenesses, manners and customs are portrayed with more accuracy and truth . . . by Catlin than in all the other drawings and representations on the face of the earth," Webster stated. "I look upon it as a thing more important to us than the ascertaining of the South Pole, or anything that can be discovered in the Dead Sea or the River Jordan." But Webster's eloquence failed to convince the government to buy the paintings. Penniless, bankrupt, and depressed, Catlin sold the collection to a boilermaker in Philadelphia who stored it away in his cellar. Catlin then fled to Paris where at least King Louis Philippe and Baudelaire had accorded him recognition. The primitive world he had tried to save was being torn apart by the white man; the Indian was making his last futile attempt to stave off extinction; and his paintings and arguments were considered the daubings of a charlatan and the fantasies of a madman.

After fourteen years as a showman he had little desire to start painting again. In the Bibliothèque Impériale he read of legendary gold mines lost in the Crystal Mountains of northern Brazil. Once more in search of adventure, but now old and deaf, he set out for the jungles of South America. The saga of his new adventures overshadows anything he had ever done before. Starting from Venezuela, he traveled by canoe up the teeming Orinoco and Essequibo rivers, then on foot, across the rocky ridges of the Crystal Mountains, searching in vain for the lost mines. What he had been seeking he never found, but he gained something better, the rebirth of his inspiration, for once again he was in an unspoiled primitive wilderness, peopled only by wildlife and Indians, and once more he took up his brush.

He found a companion—a muscular, six-foot-two-inch-tall Negro, Caesar Bolla, who had escaped from slavery in Havana. Caesar carried Catlin's paints and canvas, and his broad back even served as an easel for Catlin in the jungle. Together the old, deaf, white painter and the huge, black, escaped slave wandered across thousands of miles of wilderness, more tortuous and primitive than anything Catlin had ever seen in the wildest stretches of North America. They visited scores of tribes, many of whom had never before seen either white man or Negro.

Between 1853 and 1858 they crossed the entire jungle interior

George Catlin made a number of studies of Indian tribesmen as he traveled through South America. COURTESY OF THE AMERICAN MUSEUM OF NATURAL HISTORY

of Brazil, traveled up the Amazon to its source, crossed the Andes to the coast of Peru, crossed the pampas of Argentina, the Mato Grosso, and the Tierra del Fuego, sailed around the coast of South America in a small boat—and visited more South American primitive tribes than any other white man on record, before or since. Theirs was an adventure and an association more remarkable than that of Robinson Crusoe and his man Friday— and Robinson Crusoe was a work of pure fiction!

Nor did his adventures stop there. Catlin and Caesar continued their travels, up along the entire West Coast of North America to the Aleutian Islands and across the Bering Strait to Siberia. Then back they went, on foot across the Rocky Mountains from southern California to the Gulf of Mexico, then by boat to Yucatán, where, at the town of Sisal, after five years of incredible adventures, Catlin and Caesar parted company.

Catlin went back to Paris to complete his new paintings, to repaint early pictures from memory, and to publish books defending his honor as an artist and explorer. But bad luck plagued him. His adventures were too incredible to be believable—the settlers and soldiers driving against the Indians, stealing their lands, and sacking their villages had not found a warm and hospitable welcome, but savage, unrelenting warfare. When, after thirty-one years of absence, Catlin finally returned to New York to exhibit his pictures, he was overwhelmed by competition from P. T. Barnum, the greatest showman of them all, and once more ignored and scorned.

Penniless and destitute, frustrated in all his dreams, ambitions, objectives, and aims, he died in 1872 at the age of seventy-seven. In 1873, Joseph Henry, director of the Smithsonian Institution, wrote: "They [Catlin's paintings] will grow in importance with the passing years, and when the race of which they are the representation shall have entirely disappeared, their value will be inestimable." Seven years too late for Catlin to enjoy it, vindication came when his original collection was rescued from the boilermaker's cellar in Philadelphia and given a permanent home at the Smithsonian Institution in Washington.

Catlin's lifetime of adventure and achievement is the most amazing phenomenon in American art.

THE ROBBER BARONS

By the end of the 1850s the nation had grown into a mighty union, despite problems that indicated civil war was fast approaching. The slogan and dream of manifest destiny were a reality by mid-century. To the Capitol in Washington, D.C., came the legislators of a nation that stretched unbroken from the Atlantic to the Pacific. It was a nation mighty in size, but split deep and wide, not only by differences in geography and climate, but by ways of life and social values. The industrial North attracted wave upon wave of immigrants. Agriculture dominated the South, where population grew slowly, and slaves, rather than machines, turned the wheels.

As the country spread westward, political and economic differences between North and South widened. Daniel Webster's proposal that the government buy George Catlin's Indian collection was defeated by the Southern majority whose members looked on the Western lands as a logical area for the expansion of slavery and voted down the pur-

A contemporary cartoon by F. Opper was highly critical of the leading industrialists of the day

chase to avoid creating sympathy for the Indians, who would be displaced. The Kansas War, the Dred Scott Decision, the publication of *Uncle Tom's Cabin,* the breakup of the Whig Party, the Underground Railroad were all signs pointing the way to war—or separation—the inevitables against which Lincoln argued in vain.

When the Civil War began, the North had a population of 19 million—almost twice that of the South's 6.5 million white people and 3.5 million slaves. The North was industrially advanced and could produce all the materials it needed. The South, lacking munitions, shipyards, supplies, transportation, industry, metalworking plants, was subject to blockade and starvation—and suffered grievously from both.

It was a war of the muzzle loader and smoothbore, a war fought before the invention of smokeless powder, with battlefields so shrouded with clouds of smoke that even commanders had little idea of what had transpired until long after their fates had been decided. Casualties were astronomical. In proportion to population, casualties were greater than those suffered by either the British or the French during World War I. The North admitted to 93,443 dead on the battlefield or from combat injuries—and 210,400 from disease! There were no official estimates of Confederate losses, but battle must have claimed at least 90,000 and disease and starvation another 180,000. Thus, from a population of 31 million, 540,000 Americans died. Despite the slaughter, American expansion roared ahead through immigration and accelerated birthrate. Between 1860 and 1870 the population increased by more than 8 million.

The emancipation of the American woman began during the Civil War. From the high point of her cultural and social independence in prerevolutionary colonial days, she had gradually been pushed backward into the kitchen until, at the beginning of the Civil War, she was not even acceptable as a nurse. But Dorothea Dix fought her way through to enlistment as a nurse, and three thousand women followed her example and volunteered, doing what they could to help the wounded while simultaneously firing the first shots in the war between the sexes that ended with the victory of female suffrage.

Northern industry expanded at runaway speeds. In Philadelphia alone, 180 new factories were built and equipped between 1862 and 1864. New machines were invented—the Howe sewing machine, the McKay shoe machine, and the reaper, which made farming an industry. Petroleum was discovered in Pennsylvania in 1859, and production increased in only three years from 84,000 to 128 million gallons. Kerosene replaced candles and whale oil, and cheap glass lamps were manufactured and distributed by the millions. Never before had the homes of America been so brightly illuminated. Immigration during the five years of the war added 800,000 people to the national census.

The Homestead Act—passed in 1862, giving 160 acres to any man for a small fee and the fortitude to settle it—stimulated a new wave of westward migration, and before the war was over, 25 million acres had been claimed. In 1859 the Colorado gold rush was on—it was Pikes Peak or bust! In 1861, Colorado, Dakota, and Nevada became territories, and Kansas was granted statehood. Nevada added a star to the flag in 1864. At least 300,-000 immigrants crossed the plains to California and Oregon—seeking gold and an escape from the draft and the war.

Production of pork, wool, wheat, corn almost tripled. Europe, at peace but suffering from poor harvests, in 1862 imported 40 million bushels of wheat and flour from the war-torn United States. Profitable and normal activities continued in the urban North. In Washington, Lincoln wielded greater power than any president before him and all who followed until Franklin Delano Roosevelt.

In Newport, on fashionable Long Island, in Saratoga Springs —social functions went along as usual, only with more gaiety and lavishness. Horse racing became a popular sport for those growing rich on the war's profits. In New York, P. T. Barnum staged entertainment extravaganzas that drew huge crowds, while Catlin's show, telling the truth about the slaughter of the Indians, drew yawns and empty seats. With a war on, college enrollment dropped off a bit, but educators, sensing the future, established new colleges—Vassar, Massachusetts Institute of Technology, La Salle, Bates, Swarthmore, Cornell, and the University of Maine.

Harvard and Yale celebrated Grant's siege of Petersburg by resuming their crew races and all the elaborate social activities that accompanied them—and those families with enough money or the proper social position could buy their sons out of the draft, quite legally.

Magazines continued to publish in the North, and writers were in great demand. The standards and formats of *Harper's Weekly, The Atlantic Monthly, The North American Review,* and the *Scientific American* surpassed anything they had ever been before. And a new weekly, *The Nation,* was launched.

In the South the war was total, absorbing everything. The economic and political structure was a chain of weaknesses, with transportation the most fragile link. Although the South had sufficient railroad equipment at the beginning of the war, lack of manufacturing facilities, bottlenecks, battles, and breakdowns stopped the wheels from turning and prevented the replacement of outworn or destroyed parts. This was a new era—armies moved on ribbons of steel rather than on foot.

Slavery was not the only issue, but it was the most important one. The South was unquestionably for it; in the North the issue and the attitudes weren't quite so clear-cut. After the Emancipation Proclamation was signed, great speeches were written and delivered, and sincere efforts were made to form Negro units to serve in the army. Negro units from Massachusetts wrote some of the war's most gallant history, and a Negro corps formed in Louisiana in 1862 distinguished itself on the battle-fields despite a congressional decision that a white private was worth thirteen dollars a month, but the risk of the life of a Negro of equal rank was worth only six.

More books have been written about the Civil War than any other war in mankind's history. It has been called the American Epic, the American Iliad. It marked the triumph of Federalism, the emergence of the modern president, the rise of industrial America, the end of slavery. But although Mathew Brady recorded it on film with sharpness, precision, and accuracy, and Winslow Homer illustrated it in vivid color and dramatic line for an anxious public at home, its effect on the nation's art was almost negligible. As far as painting was concerned, the war was an interruption, little else.

After five years it was all over; suddenly Abraham Lincoln was dead, and there was no one to carry forward his humane program for reunification. The North had won the war, but the South, determined that the region should forever be white man's country, set about winning the peace. Slavery was lost—but not its spirit and essence. Despite the economic plight of the South, the plantations survived for their owners, and wealth was waiting only to be planted and harvested. At first there was neither capital nor currency. The banks were insolvent, the shops empty of goods, the schools destroyed. But the land was there, and as the men straggled back from the battlefields, they took up their hoes and plows to keep their families from starving.

Gradually, as in colonial days, tobacco emerged as the salvation of the South. Washington Duke and his family turned all their thousands of North Carolina acres to the growth and production of tobacco—and the aristocratic Reynolds family forsook King Cotton to set up a factory for the manufacture of "smokes and snuff for the public."

By 1877 all the former Confederate States were back in the Union, seated in the chamber of the House of Representatives that Samuel Morse had painted, propounding the patriotic sentiments Trumbull had portrayed in the rotunda, helping run the Union, in complete charge of their own domestic affairs, and enjoying the benefits of a new slow growth of industrialization.

Mark Twain called the years after the Civil War the "Gilded Age." These were the years of the fast dollar. The middle-class man tried to join the parade of new millionaires and often was poorer for his efforts. Stock speculation, overproduction, overextension of credit, overrapid expansion of the West, the worldwide drop in prices—all had their effect. There was a panic in 1873, and three years of depression followed while the Robber Barons grew richer, the middle class sewed patches onto their torn clothes and started planning again—and the poor got poorer.

The Civil War had tremendous impact on the economy of the country. Transportation was the keystone, providing the structure for industrial change. There were 35,000 miles of steam railroad in the United States in 1865; by 1900 there was more than five times that amount—more track than in all of Europe. A golden railroad spike had been driven in 1869 in honor of the joining of the Central Pacific and the Union Pacific near Salt Lake City. By 1870 a passenger could board a train in Boston and emerge ten days later in San Francisco.

Railroading was the big business of this era, contributing to everything else that came along—electric machines, the type-writer, the telephone, bicycles, the adding machine, fountain pen, the five-and-ten-cent store, the thresher, the harvester, the elevator, the skyscraper. The first elevated railway in the world was con-structed in New York City. Electric lights began to replace kerosene and gas lamps. The Brooklyn Bridge spanned New York's East River. The first commercial telephone exchange was opened. Cable cars ran through the streets of San Francisco, and trolley cars rumbled through Richmond. With trains flying across the land on steel rails and messages flashing from coast to coast through copper wires, the frontier disappeared. The era of mercantilism that had begun with European settlements in 1607 was dead—but not the tradition of the Puritans. That may have been driven underground, but it was there, waiting only its chance to emerge in a more favorable atmosphere.

For better or for worse, the millionaire was America's hero in the decades between Lincoln and Woodrow Wilson. His pomp and manners were admired by the millions who hoped without hope, of living in his palace and in his manner. He set the style, for art, culture, architecture, literature. Rags to riches became the American mythology—"Barefoot Newsboy Makes Good!"

In 1872 tentative income taxes imposed during the Civil War were repealed, giving still more power and money to the rich. And just in case Congress got any democratic ideas, in 1894 Joseph H. Choate, a lawyer, persuaded the Supreme Court that income taxes— graduated so that the wealthy paid more than the poor—were unconstitutional, and still more money poured into the homes that mirrored the magnificence of the rich. Not until 1913 did the Sixteenth Amendment gain ratification—and in these taxless years the merchant princes, the Robber Barons, and their Age of Elegance thrived—in magnificent palaces that rivaled the castles of the Medici family of the Italian Renaissance.

As their mansions grew, so did their horizons. More and more Americans joined the Grand Tour to Europe. With much money and little culture they sailed across the Atlantic, glided into museums because it was the thing to do, visited castles, cathedrals, palaces, and manor houses—sought and bought, admired and memorized materials and ideas of monuments and places, using a new tool and plaything, the camera. Wherever the American went, he photographed. At just the period when European influence on American architecture was at its height, the camera was perfected—and the mansion hunters brought back accurate, identifiable ideas in photographs—not vague memory images that were often blurred and distorted.

Wealthy Americans wanted mansions and museums of their own to house and display the grandeur that had been the Old World's and was now theirs. In building them they combined all styles, periods, and places—sometimes with taste, more often without. And when their buildings were completed, they turned to painting and sculpture. They invaded the art markets of Europe, carrying back to America masterpieces by Raphael, Titian, Turner.

The period between the Civil War and the turn of the century has been called by many names—the Age of Elegance, the Gilded Age, the Years of the Robber Barons, the Gay Nineties, the Victorian Age—none of these really conveys the confusion, romanticism, picturesqueness, and general bad taste that characterized that era.

The middle class did not have wealth, but it did have aspirations. Thus the example set by the upper classes, who photographed, copied, and adapted every motif, form, and style European aristocracy ever had, was followed by the newly rich merchants, manufacturers, and shopkeepers of the middle class. Unaccustomed to luxury, they often mistook ostentation for elegance.

For them, the jigsaw was the greatest invention of the age, making possible all manner of shaped wooden posts and decorations. Who needed a sculptor? Any competent carpenter could cut out any shape a man's mind could imagine—scrolls, lacework, dentils. Short, light, delicate gingerbread designs began to adorn eaves, windows, and doors, inside and out. The turning lathe added to the confusion, spewing out rounded wooden posts by the thousands to hold up the roofs of the porches demanded by the Victorians. Curiously, as the houses presented the world with elaborate façades, the owners sought refuge under the protective roofs of the porches that spanned much of the lower story. Indeed, the house spoke for itself in lavish and spectacular tones, while the owners, as if guided by rules of etiquette and modest behavior, retired modestly into the shadows of their porches.

As foundries grew in number, cast iron was used for balconies and trim—and a cast iron animal rooted to the ground on the front lawn became the height of style.

If any one style ruled the day, it was Gothic. Americans avidly read medieval tales and poems. The Victorian English couple, Elizabeth Barrett Browning and her husband Robert Browning, were among the nation's most popular writers, and Alfred Lord Tennyson's *Idylls of the King* appeared in one volume in 1869 and immediately became a best seller.

Elaborate embellishments covered the interiors of buildings as well as the exteriors. Rooms were crammed with furniture, bric-a-brac, vases, pictures, fat leather-upholstered furniture, iron-ware, Tiffany glass, Persian rugs.

Many houses were built with a porte-cochere, a rooflike extension that jutted outward from the side of the house and spanned the driveway to protect visitors from the rain as they alighted from their carriages. In a sense, this structure is the ancestor of the carport, so common to many of our homes today.

Wide flights of steps led into these mansions, and more flights led to upstairs stories. Patterned and flowered wallpaper covered all the walls, and the floors wore as many different carpets as the lady of the house wore petticoats. Windows were covered with curtains of lace and draperies of satin and velvet that cut off both light and air. Dark wood trim and paneling contributed to the somber effect—to the so-called golden patina of the Victorian atmosphere.

Life centered in the dining room, around a heavy, unmoving table and gigantic, uncomfortable chairs. The kitchen was removed, a respectable, inconvenient distance away. In keeping with Victorian tastes, unpleasant sights and sounds were hidden —at all costs, even efficiency. Victorians were intriguing people— on the one hand modest, even prudish—fastidious, correct, and decorous. On the other hand they were overdressed, overhoused, overfurnished, and enthusiastic for exaggeration in all directions.

Industrialization set the tempo for the Victorian Age. Mills and factories changed from private to trust ownership. Everything grew bigger. New industrial empires required factories that covered acres of land. Thousands of workers required thousands of homes, and speculators filled block after block of the metropolitan areas with rows of attached houses and apartments. Before long apartment dwellers outnumbered homeowners, and the average man bought his house ready-made. Only the rich could afford architects—and they grew as wealthy as their clients.

By the end of the nineteenth century the worst horrors of housekeeping were ended. Municipal water systems brought pure water into the house, and the old cistern, well, and pump disappeared. Modern plumbing carried hot and cold water all over the house—gone were the backyard washpots, the tubs, and the fires. Central heating became standard. The untidy woodpile gave way to the basement fuel bin, the hidden gas pipe, the buried oil tank. Electric lighting eliminated the last sooty lamp chimney and faulty gas mantle . . . American civilization was in full flower.

The Victorian house and art and way of life have gone out of style. Only a few remnants remain of one of the most picturesque periods of American history. But the Puritan house, the Puritan portrait, built and painted for the common man, remain—still vital influences on our building and art.

[9]

THE AMERICAN MASTERS: THOSE WHO STAYED

The most non-Victorian painters of the era, more aware of the emerging forces of the future than the romantic and classical traditions of the past, became the great American masters of the Victorian period. Winslow Homer and Thomas Eakins ignored the artificialities, the gingerbread, the booming abundance and shams of their generation and sought truth and clarity, light and substance. They pursued rugged, self-imposed Puritan traditions and achieved lasting greatness. But, as with most nonconformists—including the majority of their contemporaries among the Impressionist artists of France—fame came too late for their enjoyment.

Both artists went abroad, but unlike Copley who remained in England and Cole who deserted his traditions, Homer and Eakins returned with their visions of America strengthened and sharpened, to view the life and landscape about them in unshakable American terms.

Objective realism and ruthlessly factual interpretation were the grounds on which both men found failure and fame. Walt Whitman said

Detail. "Prisoners from the Front" by Winslow Homer. THE METROPOLITAN MUSEUM OF ART, GIFT OF MRS. FRANK B. PORTER, 1922

of Thomas Eakins: "I never knew of but one artist, and that's Tom Eakins, who could resist the temptation to see what they thought ought to be, rather than what is."

Winslow Homer said simply, "I am just a reporter." And this description of him was echoed by a contemporary critic for the *Art Journal* who wrote: "He paints what he has seen. He tells what he has felt. He records what he knows."

Another contemporary, Henry James, who was one of the most respected and perceptive critics of the day wrote of Homer: "He not only has no imagination . . . he is almost barbarously simple, and, to our eye, he is horribly ugly."

Lloyd Goodrich, director of the Whitney Museum, who views Homer through the lenses of history, is far more gentle: "Homer looked more at nature than at other art, painted by eye, rather than tradition."

Both men turned from old concepts to blaze new trails. Homer made watercolor a medium for great paintings rather than merely the material for preliminary sketches. He handled it with dash and vigor, without the preliminary line drawing that was the standard procedure of the time. In a period when most water-colorists overloaded their works with cluttering detail, Homer suggested more by painting less, utilizing the sweeping brush-strokes and crisp washes that were all but impossible to attain with any other medium. And Eakins, teaching at the Pennsyl-vania Academy of Fine Arts, substituted live models for plaster casts. Instead of having his students make careful preliminary drawings, he recommended direct application of the loaded brush, drawing with color rather than thinking of a painting as a colored drawing. "The outline," he said, "is not the man . . . Paint! . . . complicated things are thus reduced to simple things!"

Similar as the two artists were, they were also quite different. Homer was a dandy—slender, erect, with an enormous handlebar moustache, dark eyes, high cheekbones. As a young man he dressed in the style of the day—in loud checks, high collars, and bowler hats—and in his sixties, according to the director of the Pennsylvania Academy of Fine Arts, "He was the essence of gentlemanly elegance . . . he might have been taken for a successful stockbroker." While Eakins, unconcerned about others' opinions, without polish or refinement, was a direct, blunt, hard, and tactless man, careless in dress and appearance.

Homer gave up city life and depiction of the human image as he grew older. He settled down at Prouts' Neck along the wild, rocky coast of Maine where he painted the power, strength, and majesty of the sky and shifting moods of nature. Though he lived in New York City for twenty years before moving to Maine, he never painted a New York scene. It was not until he was sixty that his art reached its true greatness and gained the acceptance of artists and critics.

Eakins never really forsook Philadelphia and its people. He focused his art and teaching on the human figure, finding his great themes in portraits and in the contemporary life of his region—rowing on the river, bird-shooting in the marshes, sailing on the Delaware, relaxing at home. As he grew older, rebuffs and lack of recognition sapped Eakins' vitality; his work became

"Northeaster" by Winslow Homer. THE METROPOLITAN MUSEUM OF ART, GIFT OF GEORGE A. HEARN, 1910

increasingly sterile and repetitious while he withdrew from the objective world that had rejected him. As Homer improved, Eakins declined.

Eakins was a professor of drawing and painting at the Pennsylvania Academy of Fine Arts, a lecturer on anatomy, an advocate of disciplined and realistic drawing from the living figure. He established a solid artistic foundation in his students. As a student, Eakins first studied at the academy, then went to the École des Beaux-Arts in Paris to work with the leading academicians of France. He became the favorite pupil of Gérôme and worked so intensely he became ill. He went to Spain to recover, and during his seven months there he studied and learned still more from the works of the seventeenth-century artists Velázquez and Ribera.

Homer had little formal training. He began his career as an illustrator of popular weeklies and magazines. When he did go to France, he tramped the streets of Paris, painted a few scenes in the country—and managed to remain remarkably uninfluenced by French painters. "If a man wants to be an artist," he once said, "he should never look at pictures." He followed his own advice by ignoring the paintings in the Louvre and concentrating his attentions on the pretty French girl copyists.

According to Lloyd Goodrich, "If any artist in modern times can be called self-made, it was he [Homer]."

In general, Homer spoke little about art—his own or the work of anybody else. Prospective purchasers would be referred to his dealers in New York and Boston, and when he did answer an inquiry, it was brusque and businesslike. "I can offer you only water colors. I have them from Canada, Bermuda, Bahamas, Florida and the coast of Maine. They always net me $175 each, no frames, no matter the size; they are mostly 14 x 21. Do you think you would like any of them sent to you on immediate approval for cash? If so, what country would you like represented? Hurry up—as it's very cold here!"

Contrast Homer's Yankee practicality and flintiness with the attitude of Eakins who answered a dissatisfied sitter's request for

"Sloop, Bermuda" by Winslow Homer. THE METROPOLITAN MUSEUM OF
ART, AMELIA B. LAZARUS FUND, 1910

a lower price with the statement "I cannot bring myself to re-
gard this affair in the light of a business transaction."

Homer's people were types rather than individuals, and their
activities were more important than their physical appearances.
He painted nature "exactly as it appears," never seeking to express subjective emotions but only the true and powerful images
of the real world that stirred him. Eakins gave his figures an
expressive force, power, and inner vitality that made them come
alive on canvas. His people were imbued with a spirit of life,
often in contemplative mood and viewed with compassionate
understanding. The critic Daniel Mendelowitz writes of Eakins:
"Walt Whitman looks out of his portrait—expansive, optimistic,
dishevelled—loving the world yet not quite able to face its uncompromising realities. Eakins saw and painted the tender poet
underneath the blustering exterior."

Recognition and modest patronage came to Homer during his

lifetime, though critics continued to carp about his "lack of finish." The National Academy, the Brooklyn Art Association, and the Water Color Society exhibited his work annually. He had shows in Paris, in Philadelphia at the Centennial, and in Munich. At the age of twenty-nine he was elected a full-fledged academician at the National Academy of Design, one of the youngest Americans ever to receive that honor. In 1876 his first oil painting, "Prisoners at the Front," was purchased for $1,800, a very high price at that time for a painting by a living American artist. ("Niagara Falls," painted by Frederick Church, brought $12,500 at the same sale.) Today, any one of Homer's watercolors would bring a minimum of $3,000, while "Prisoners at the Front" is valued at about $60,000, far more than "Niagara Falls." Eight gold medals eventually found their way into the dusty drawers of his Prouts Neck home.

Homer's work was prominently displayed at the Philadelphia

"Prisoners from the Front" by Winslow Homer. THE METROPOLITAN MUSEUM OF ART, GIFT OF MRS. FRANK B. PORTER, 1922

Centennial, while Eakins' "Gross Clinic," today considered to be one of his masterpieces, was refused admission to the Hall of Art and hung with medical displays, although five of his lesser works were selected by the jury. As Homer's fame increased, Eakins grew more and more strained. Long hours of tactless teaching and monumental tensions aggravated the relationship between the artist and the proper Philadelphian directors of the academy. Eakins insisted on using live models. He had even asked some of Philadelphia's most dignified Victorian matrons to pose in the nude for him. Citizens of the city never quite fully recovered from his use of nude male models posed before academy classes that were composed of both male and female students.

Thomas Eakins was born in Philadelphia in 1844. He studied, painted, lived, and died there. Philadelphia had been a city of science since the days of Ben Franklin and the Peales. Eakins, with his deep scientific interests, his painstaking studies, and firmly structured compositions, conformed perfectly to that aspect of the city's attitude.

After the short period of his studies abroad, Eakins returned to Philadelphia to turn his eye on the city and its people, sports, and recreation, its home life and scientific interests. Not since Copley had true characterization been so accurately revealed in portraiture. What Copley did for Boston's society, Eakins did for Philadelphia's. If all a client wanted was flattery, Eakins sent him elsewhere. But if he sought portrayal with compassion and a sense of human dignity, by an eye that looked beyond the conformation of features into character, experience, and thinking, Eakins was his man.

Much in the work of Eakins is reminiscent of the Dutch painters of the seventeenth century. They, too, painted simple domestic scenes with clarity, brilliance, and artistic merit, finding themes for their great works in corners of rooms, the fronts of houses, along the banks of rivers. Neither Eakins nor these Dutch masters felt a need to travel to far-off places for exotic themes. All they needed to fashion their great paintings they found in and around home and city.

Influenced in his early years by the intense dark and light contrasts in the work of Rembrandt and Ribera, Eakins sought these same dramatic effects in his own work. He painted profoundly, solidly, and accurately. He sought out scientists and college professors for his friends as well as subjects for portraits, and viewed and rendered forms and figures with an objective eye and brush. To assure his knowledge of the human form he studied anatomy, not at art school, but at the Jefferson Medical College in Philadelphia. He studied and portrayed the nude, building his figures with the precision of a surgeon wielding a scalpel.

His fascination with the scientific came to a climax in 1875 with "The Gross Clinic," a life-sized representation of the outstanding teacher and surgeon of Philadelphia. The painting, which shows Dr. Gross lecturing a class during a surgical opera-

"The Gross Clinic" by Thomas Eakins. COURTESY OF THE JEF-
FERSON MEDICAL COLLEGE, PHILADELPHIA. PHOTOGRAPHED BY PHIL-
ADELPHIA MUSEUM OF ART

tion, recalls Rembrandt's "Anatomy Lesson," more than two hundred years earlier. Eakins, in the American spirit of reality, drama, and documentation, made it a spacious scene, peopled with more figures, with more emotional impact than Rembrandt's. Dr. Gross dominates the center of the canvas, scalpel in hand, with the incised leg of the body still before him. Thoughtfully he pauses before addressing an amphitheater filled with students. His hand and scalpel smeared with blood and a student who covers his face and recoils in horror give the painting its vivid sense of drama. The canvas is huge, the figures big as life. The somber colors—contrasting lights, darks—and the precision of Eakins' style make this an American masterpiece.

But the Philadelphia Centennial refused it. The public found it "too graphic . . . emotionally disturbing . . . a despoliation of art." It was rejected and reviled, and Eakins, so shattered by this lack of appreciation for what he felt was his masterpiece, never really recovered.

Fourteen years later, in 1889, he painted another large group composition for a medical group. But the "Agnew Clinic" was neither as masterful as his earlier work, nor as ambitious.

In 1879, after having served as an assistant, Eakins became professor of drawing and painting at the Pennsylvania Academy of Fine Arts. He immediately substituted live models for the plaster casts his predecessor had preferred and advocated the revolutionary concept that painters should model in clay to gain discipline and a feeling of plasticity. His career was brief. In 1886 he was dismissed, his tactlessness before the directors and his own feelings of rejection contributing to his dismissal.

While his paintings of indoor subjects showed much of Rembrandt's passion for dark and light contrasts, his outdoor paintings gleamed with a brilliance that blazed trails the Impressionists would follow a generation later.

Asked by an interviewer for a biography, Eakins replied briefly, "My life is all in my work." If this is true, then the testimony of history, despite his rejections and failures, is inescapable: Thomas Eakins lived a magnificent life.

At his death in 1916 only three museums owned his work.

Yankee traditions were deeply ingrained in Winslow Homer. He was born in Boston in 1836, and his family had been New England traders for two centuries. At the age of nineteen he was apprenticed to a successful Boston lithographer for whom he drew pretty girls for sheet music covers. Released from indenture on his twenty-first birthday, he began receiving free-lance assignments from *Bellow's Pictorial* and *Harper's Weekly,* sketching pictures which would be reproduced as wood blocks. In 1859 *Harper's* offered him a staff job, but he turned it down. "I have had no master and shall never have any," he wrote, feeling it would fetter and restrict him. But he moved to New York to be close to the magazine's office and continued free-lancing for *Harper's* for the next seventeen years.

Homer expanded as an artist by working within the limitations of magazine reproduction—a medium that was entirely black and white and depended on rough cross-hatching for patterns of gray. He discovered that clarity of form, sharp outline, and unsubtle shadows, if used with simplicity, could have far more power and drama than countless details and blended middle tones. He discovered, too, that facial detail was not always essential and that he could achieve greater strength through pose and costume. His pictures were composed of large areas of lights and darks. He gained atmospheric effect by silhouetting dark figures against background lights. The techniques he learned in working for the wood engravers were carried over into his painting.

Homer's art grew from a base of solid, precise drawing, clear observation, an innate sense of color harmony, and complete control of his medium, whether lithographer's crayon, oil paints, or watercolors. Technical precision and masculine energy mark his work.

His first magazine assignments were to illustrate text material. However, his editors soon discovered that Homer's illustrations had more appeal than the texts they were illustrating. They gave him free rein, and he chose as subjects vivid pictures of life in New York City, Newport, Long Branch, the Adirondacks, Gloucester Harbor, or any other place that caught his fancy. After

"The Sharpshooter," a wood engraving by Winslow Homer. IBM COLLECTION

the Civil War began, *Harper's* sent artist-correspondents to cover both armies in order to satisfy the public demand for news pictures. These correspondents lived with the soldiers, observed the battles, and sent back drawings and written accounts. Homer made several trips to the front, but he was not permanently assigned to the army and was a war artist only briefly.

At the age of twenty-five, Homer made his first oil painting. After a friend showed him how to set up a palette and handle his brushes, he went out to challenge the landscape. He applied his color thickly, directly, and boldly, without variations, glazes, or any of the techniques that take practice and learning. He used this method for the rest of his career, improving with such rapid strides that a mere four years after his first oil was completed he was accepted into the National Academy.

Shortly after the Civil War ended, he dressed a dummy in Union and Confederate uniforms, set it up in four different positions, and painted "Prisoners at the Front." In this painting he contrasted the character of a victorious Union officer with the grim figures of three captured rebels. Against a background of the devastated Virginia countryside, the young, neat Union officer—looking almost as if he had just stepped off the West Point parade ground—faces a bedraggled, ragtag group of Confederates, very young, very old, very bewildered, and very defiant. Homer's discipline as an illustrator is apparent in the careful drawing and posing of the figures. This, combined with unified tonality, well-ordered composition, and solidly rendered figures, made this painting a sensation when it was exhibited at the National Academy of Design in 1866. It was the most highly acclaimed painting to come out of the Civil War. One critic went so far as to hail it as the most vivid and powerful depiction of war ever painted. If Homer never again had committed brush to canvas, this painting alone would have assured his fame.

"Prisoners at the Front" and another of Homer's paintings were included in a selection of American art sent to the Paris Universal Exposition in 1867. Homer went along to receive the accolades of the critics and stayed until he ran out of money ten months later.

Completely uninfluenced by his stay in Europe, he launched into American genre painting, portraying woodsmen, soldiers, milkmaids, campfire scenes, hunters, fishermen, children, pretty girls. He caught the spirit of American people and their setting in a unique and intimate atmosphere. Homer lived in New York City but retreated from it in his painting, working from memory and sketches of summer scenes in the country. Country life and country people became his theme. Still the public was largely unresponsive. As Homer turned more and more to simplicity and truth, the public moved further and further toward Victorian excess. Despite the recognition and acclaim of art critics, his work did not sell. Perhaps because he did not glamorize or attempt to improve on people or nature but portrayed things as they were, his paintings did not appeal to the tastes of the times. He found it necessary to continue illustrating for *Harper's* in order to earn his livelihood.

Early in the 1870s he began experimenting with monochromatic watercolor washes in an effort to achieve a more naturalistic feeling in his wood blocks. The move from one color on a block of wood to many colors on paper was an easy and natural development. By 1873, he began working seriously in watercolor.

Cautiously, at first with a line drawing to support his colored forms, and then, as he discovered the versatility of the medium, with bold, fresh, clear washes—with rich and vibrant lights that projected spark and intensity. Many of Homer's paintings achieved a monumentality and grandeur that belied their small size.

At last he had a medium with which he could work directly out-of-doors without returning to the studio to complete a composition—a medium that allowed him to produce more pictures for less expensive prices. By 1874, he gave up wood-block illustrations for painting in oil and watercolors.

However, he still ran counter to popular tastes. His oil paintings, handled with the broad, expressive freedom of watercolors, were considered unfinished sketches. His naturalism was called ugliness. (In Europe, at just about the same time, the Impressionists encountered the same criticism.) Homer railed against the critics' smug views and verbal attacks. "For fifteen years the press has called me a promising young artist," he wrote. "I'm tired of it!" As for the public, he hung a sign on his studio door reading "Coal bin."

Discouraged by the lack of appreciation, at the age of forty-five he left New York and went to Europe to spend two years painting at Tynemouth on England's bleak North Sea coast.

When he returned to America in 1881, it was not to New York but to Prouts' Neck in Maine. Prouts' Neck is ten miles south of Portland, on a rocky peninsula that juts out into the cold Atlantic. Homer had spent summer vacations there at his brother's cottage in the past. Now he made it his home. A bleak, rocky moor, dense with undergrowth, it was populated only by fishermen and poor dirt farmers. Today it is an exclusive summer resort. On this granite-ribbed coast he observed, studied, and absorbed the spirit of the sea and rocks. No other American, indeed, possibly no other artist, had ever painted the roaring tides, the onrushing waves, the storm-worn boulders, and the fogbound shores with such power, drama, and love, or had ever conveyed the movement and dynamics of the sea with such intense emotion. As Homer became attuned to the Maine coast, his paintings grew larger in size and reflected the battle of man against the forces of nature—a reflection of his own futile conflicts with the critics.

"I do my own work," he wrote a friend. "No other man or woman within half a mile, and four miles from the railroad or post office. This is the only life in which I am permitted to mind my own business. . . . I like my home more than ever as people thin out."

Winters were wild, cold, lonely, and rigorous, with northeasters driving the waves in roaring cascades against the granite cliffs. Homer's studio was a simple house; an iron stove provided only enough heat to make two rooms habitable in winter. His walls were his notebook. He covered them with numbers, sketches, and reminders. He chopped and melted ice for his water, did his own cooking, associated with the simple fisherfolk or no one at all, and kept a boat in one of his heated rooms to make it impossible for use by guests. Early to bed and early to rise governed his life.

"I deny that I am a recluse," he wrote a friend. "Neither am I an unsociable hog. I am perfectly happy and contented."

Years later, just before his fifty-ninth birthday, Homer wrote to his brother that "The life that I have chosen gives me full hours of enjoyment for the balance of my life. The sun will not rise, or set, without my notice, and thanks."

He left Prouts' Neck for long vacations, some summers to the Adirondacks and the Canadian woods, some winters to the Bahamas and Bermuda. He left his oils behind and took only his watercolors. He gave this medium an amazingly youthful zest—in form, movement, and color—and produced works that rank him among the greatest watercolorists in Western art. For several years he maintained a small studio in New York City, traveling there occasionally when he needed models other than Prouts Neck could provide.

It was from the granite-bound inhospitable cliffs of Maine that Homer focused his reporter's eye on the sea and the men who wrested their living from it. He told of their strength and courage, of their will as indomitable as the cliffs themselves, of their work and danger, of their never-ending struggle for survival. He loved the wildest, most solitary aspects of nature—the sea, the forest, the mountains, and the hardy breed of men who inhabited them.

But it was to his Tenth Street studio in New York that he came in 1884 to complete "The Lifeline," the painting that marked the second landmark of public and critical acclaim in his career. In this violent drama, two water-soaked, frightened figures move across the space of his canvas, dangling from two ropes, stretching from an unseen wreck to unknown safety. Waves pound the distant cliffs. An unconscious woman is held by a rescuer, whose face is obscured by the woman's blowing scarf.

Homer posed his models on the roof of his studio, using the sky's cloudy glow for his light and dippers full of water for his wet reality, to produce a drenched, robust couple—the woman feminine, curved, and gentle, in need of and receiving protection —but without the saccharine sentimentality so typical of the Victorian era. "If you want more sentimentality put into this picture," Homer wrote his dealer, "I can, with one or two touches, give it a stomach ache that will suit any customer."

The drama and excitement of "The Lifeline" brought more than public attention and unanimous critical acclaim. Exhibited in the National Academy of Design show in 1884, it was purchased by the collector Catharine Lorillard Wolfe for $2,500—the first American painting in her collection.

As Homer grew older, he turned less and less frequently to the image of man for subject matter, concentrating instead on the age-old struggle between ocean and rock. "The Northeaster," painted in 1895, a simple, dynamic composition of waves, spray, rock, and sky, reached heights of solidity, grandeur, and monumentality that have been imitated by many painters but never equaled. In creating his own vision of the world, he captured the essence of the American landscape—the wilderness and the men who are part of it—and his works remain a testament to America.

What Delacroix stands for in the art of France, or Gainsborough in the art of England, Winslow Homer represents to America.

It was Cézanne who said of Monet, "He is an eye—but what an eye!" The same can be said of Winslow Homer and Thomas Eakins, two of America's great Victorian Age masters.

The scientific traditions of Philadelphia contributed to American art still another objectively realistic and ruthlessly factual painter.

William Michael Harnett was born in Ireland but grew up in Philadelphia. His work, like Eakins', was related in theme and style to seventeenth-century Dutch traditions. Harnett's realism, which derived in the beginning from the still lifes of Raphael and James Peale, went far beyond that of these earlier Philadelphians to reach into a new dimension of illusionism called *trompe l'oeil* (to deceive the eye).

Harnett studied engraving as a youth; until the age of twenty-seven he earned his living as a silver engraver while attending night classes in drawing at the Pennsylvania Academy of Fine Arts and later in New York at both the National Academy of Design and Cooper Union. In 1875 he made his first tentative attempts with oils, and the next year, when the silver engraving trade hit a slump that put him out of work, he went back to Philadelphia and set himself up in the business of painting still lifes.

He preferred worn and picturesque household items—newspapers, hats, writing tables, pipes, beer mugs, books, pens, old paper money—which he arranged in tight little compositions, frankly derived from the Peales but nevertheless quite personal and unique. By 1880 he had earned enough money from the sales of his paintings to travel to Europe. He stayed for six years, primarily in Munich, supporting himself by the sale of still lifes and learning a rich and mature use of his medium.

Returning to the United States in 1886, he settled in New York and continued to paint still lifes, but with a luminosity and control of textures that he could now sustain with remarkable precision even in paintings that measured as large as six by four feet. He gave up tabletop groupings and quite often developed illusionistic compositions vertically, with forms and objects suspended from a door. The wood grain, hinges, and hardware provided a rich background of color and texture for the objects attached to the door or hanging from it. So great was his love for texture and common objects, and so deep his delight with the quality and feel of pigment, that his paintings took on a haunting quality of mystery and deep emotionality.

Interestingly enough, in the past few years there has been a strong revival of interest in Harnett's paintings—probably

"Old Models" by William Michael Harnett. COURTESY, MUSEUM OF FINE ARTS, BOSTON. CHARLES HENRY HAYDEN FUND

brought about by the emergence of pop art, which is not just a portrayal of things as they are, but an intensification of life and reality. Modern critics find comparable qualities in Harnett's work.

But his own generation admired Harnett for his fantastic technique, for the fact that one could read the newspapers depicted in his paintings or could hardly be restrained from reaching out to pick up his objects. He was a master technician and magician as an illusionist. He answered every question that appeared on nature's surface; he was praised for this quality that was probably the least of his abilities as an artist and ignored for the masterful organization of shapes, color, and space that set him apart. His work and his reputation came surging back to popularity in 1947, long after the Victorian nonessentials that had made him popular in his own time had worn off.

10

The objective realists were not the only American artists who spurned the boom and bombast, sentiment and gingerbread of the Victorian Era. Other artists, seeking the inventive, the capricious, and the exquisite, spurned not only the culture of America but the land as well. As Americans before them had done, they sought Europe for their inspiration—and as no other Americans had done before them, they found much of it in the art of Japan.

In 1853 Commodore Perry's big black warships had sailed into the harbors of Japan, starting the process that unlocked the gates of feudalism and opened that ancient and exotic civilization to the modern world. By 1862 Japanese embassies were established in Europe, and soon the Impressionists were collecting and being influenced by their wood-block prints.

James A. McNeill Whistler and Mary Cassatt joined the Impressionists to help enrich this extraordinarily brilliant period in Europe. Cassatt, American born, considered herself an American to the very end, despite

THE AMERICAN MASTERS: THOSE WHO LEFT

"Girl in a Japanese Kimono" by *James McNeill Whistler*. FREER GALLERY OF ART, WASHINGTON, D.C.

a lifetime of work in France. But she is one of very few Americans to be included in histories of European art. Whistler, also American by birth, considered nationalism in art as ridiculous and preferred to be known as a universal artist, despite the fact that England regards him as one of her great nineteenth-century painters.

Working in Europe, out of touch with the taste and traditions of America, under the influence of European modern artists and centuries-old Japanese decorative patterns, these artists created a current in American art that outlived the Victorian Era that had produced them. Their work was far more faithful to the American Puritan tradition than the gaudy paintings of lesser artists that had such popular appeal at the time. Indeed, of all the influences of the Victorian Era on American art today, it was the work and personalities of the expatriates Whistler and Cassatt that is most profound.

Whistler created the cult of Bohemianism among artists and first voiced the philosophy of "art for art's sake"—the belief that color, patterns, and forms are fundamental objectives in painting and far more important than merely illustrating history, literature, man, and the forms of nature. Cassatt, a member of a wealthy and prominent Philadelphia family, was influential in shaping American taste by inducing wealthy American collectors to buy the works of her Impressionist friends. The Havemeyer collection at the Metropolitan Museum of Art is a notable example.

James A. McNeill Whistler was born in Connecticut in 1834. His father, a former army major, had resigned to take up the world-traveling career of a civil engineer and passed along his wanderlust to his artist son. From 1842 to 1849 the boy lived in St. Petersburg, Russia, where his father had been commissioned to build the railroad to Moscow. There he studied drawing at the Academy of Fine Arts. Later, on his return to the United States, with his father properly decorated by Emperor Nicholas I, he received instruction in art at West Point.

Whistler, unlike his father, grandfather, and uncles, was not cut out to be a dedicated army man. He was seventeen when he entered West Point and he hated military discipline from the moment of his arrival. Constantly in trouble, mainly for insubordination and for drawing unsympathetic caricatures of his officers, he was dropped after three trying years.

His family found him a job with the U. S. Coast and Geodetic Survey where he learned the technique of etching for drawing maps and plans. Caricatures of superiors drawn on margins of his maps drew a fast reaction, and after three months he was fired. He was twenty-one when he left for Europe, never to return to the United States.

During his first two years abroad he studied art in Paris. As unlike a Puritan as one can imagine, he still had instantaneous receptivity to new ideas and the ability to improvise that marked the first Puritan colonist who built a home out of the New England forest.

Paris was in ferment. The Impressionists were spurning and being spurned by the academy. The great Neoclassicist Ingres and

"Caprice in Purple and Gold, Number Two—The Golden Screen" by James McNeill Whistler. FREER GALLERY OF ART, WASHINGTON, D.C.

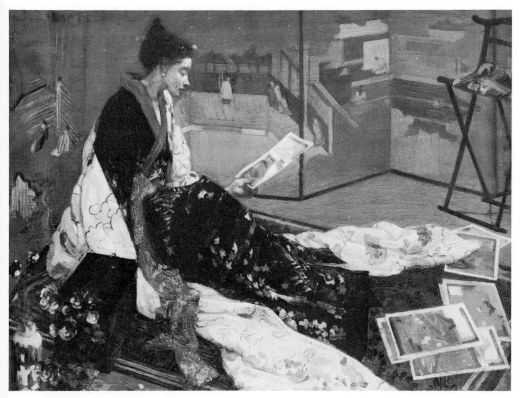

the Romanticist Delacroix were still the city's leading artists. The controversial young Courbet was preaching the revolution of objective realism. The fact that Whistler joined the revolution that sought art from ruthlessly direct observation, and not from dreams, memories, ideals, or myths, is evident in his etchings and early paintings.

When he moved to London in 1860, he brought with him many influences besides Courbet's. From the Parisians he had learned soft handling of paint. Paint, he once told a friend, should not be applied thickly but "should be like a breath on the surface of a pane of glass." From the study of Velázquez he had absorbed sober, reserved, yet powerful patterns of lights, darks, and grays, empty backgrounds, and the beauty of a long and graceful line. Above all, he had been captivated by Japanese prints that had swept through the Impressionist circles and affected the art of Toulouse-Lautrec, Degas, Cézanne, and van Gogh. Whistler absorbed the carefully arranged two-dimensional patterns of Japanese prints so unusual to Western eyes. He emulated the open, negative spaces of these prints; their off-center compositions; unexpected placing of detail; high, steep, tilted horizon or floor lines; and cool, flat colors. Whistler added a dusky darkness that made his work unique in tone, mood, and style. Grays stirred his imagination, and with them he was able to avoid the actualities and clarity of realistic life. Whereas the Impressionists worshiped brightness and sunlight, Whistler loved the mystery of twilight and evening.

One of his first full-length portraits, "The Woman in White," completed in 1862, was shown the following year at the Salon des Refuses in Paris. It was at this salon that the Impressionists showed their paintings which had been refused admission to the academy and acquired their group name from the painting "An Impression" by Monet. Together with Manet's "Luncheon on the Grass," "The Woman in White," caused the wave of shock and sensation among the critics and public that eventually shattered the temples of classical art. Quiet, muted, its colors formed broad areas; elusive and exotic, it took on the character of formal,

"The White Girl" is one of several similar full-length portraits painted by James McNeill Whistler in 1862. COURTESY OF THE NATIONAL GALLERY OF ART, WASHINGTON, D.C. HARRIS WHITTEMORE COLLECTION, 1943

decorative harmony that prompted Whistler to call his works "Nocturnes, symphonies, harmonies and arrangements."

He treated landscapes in tonal harmonies, preferring to diminish the qualities of nature and emphasize the beauty of mood, emotion, and the dark lyricism of poetry. Unlike Homer, who preferred to live with and paint in nature, Whistler abhorred the outdoors. "The country," he said, "is detestable . . . nature should always be painted at home!" He took his ideas from nature in rapid black, gray, and white sketches, and completed the "Nocturnes" in the indoor peace of his studio.

In 1871, he completed the work that was destined to go down in history as "Whistler's Mother." But Whistler called it "Arrangement in Gray and Black," and he explained, "What can, or ought the public to care about the identity of the portrait? It must stand or fall on its merits as an arrangement." His interest was in the combination of colors and patterns, not in people or objects or the story they might tell. Evidently England's Royal Academy did not think too highly of the merits of the "Arrangement." It rejected the portrait after one viewing and exhibited it only under the forceful persuasion of Whistler's friend, Sir Wil-

"Nocturne in Black and Gold: The Falling Rocket" by James McNeill Whistler. COURTESY OF THE DETROIT INSTITUTE OF ARTS

liam Boxall. The government of France purchased it for its Luxembourg Gallery in 1891, and Whistler was made an officer of the Legion of Honor.

Friends he had known in West Point who had served in the Confederate Army came to London in 1866 after the Civil War had ended. Chile and Peru were in revolt against Spain, and his friends persuaded Whistler to join them on a trip to Latin America. After a first stop in Panama, they visited Valparaíso. Whistler completed three paintings of the Valparaíso harbor before the heat of bombardment once more cooled his ardor for the military —and war of any kind—and he hastened back to London's more civilized security.

Whistler was as much showman as artist. Dapper, well-dressed, witty, sarcastic, alert, and aggressive, he was the eternal Victorian dandy. A silk hat, frock coat, yellow gloves, and long walking stick were his everyday dress—and when friends couldn't find him in his studio, they would look for him at the tailor's where he spent hours posing and preening before the mirrors. Fastidious in the most inconsequential of details, he was immaculately groomed even when he painted. Only five feet, four inches tall, with sharp, piercing blue eyes, his eyebrows thick and black, his chin prominent and pugnacious, he looked every inch the ringmaster at the circus.

In a high-pitched, strident voice that interchanged American, English, and French accents he bombarded his sitters with a constant stream of chatter while he darted back and forth during a portrait session. His palette was a whole tabletop, his brushes three feet long. He demanded perfection, and often after an entire day's work he would wipe his canvas clean and begin again. The second-rate and the inferior were not for Whistler. He sought only the best, and he drove his sitters and himself interminably. Sitters posed, fifty, eighty, as many as one hundred times, suffering anger, boredom, despair, and misery until the painting met Whistler's standards. But the artist's satisfaction did not always coincide with his patron's. "I seek to reveal character and personality," he explained haughtily, "not merely the face the model wears for that one day."

"Self Portrait" (1867) *by James McNeill Whistler.* FREER
GALLERY OF ART, WASHINGTON, D.C.

An irate sitter once complained, "You can't call that a great
work of art!"

Whistler replied crushingly, "But then, you can't call yourself
a great work of nature."

London's cultural leaders, du Maurier, Millais, Thackeray, were
lavish in their praise of Whistler. Some considered his etchings
equal to those of Rembrandt. Few artists in history other than
Rembrandt, Goya, and Dürer could equal his fame in both media
—etching and painting. But however fervent others might be
in admiration of his work, none could equal the artist's own passionate approval of himself. He heaped praise on everything he
did, much to the dismay of the English who prided themselves

on understatement and modesty. When a female admirer, in rapturous agreement with the artist's self-estimation, purred, "There are only two painters in the world, Whistler and Velázquez," Whistler shattered her with the reply, "Why drag in Velázquez?"

Entering a gallery that housed a group exhibition that included one of his own works, he strutted in humming loudly and proceeded directly to his own picture. He stood there, for fifteen minutes of silent admiration while a circle of spectators formed around him. Finally shouting, "Bravo—Jimmy!" he turned on his heel, opened a path through the crowd with his walking stick, and left without glancing at any other work.

He was a tireless host during the 1870s. To be invited to his informal, lively Sunday breakfasts was tantamount to being at the top of the intellectual and social register. His personally prepared American buckwheat cakes were the prime attraction, but lest the sophisticated and select company that never numbered fewer than ten nor more than twenty should think he was becoming provincial, he served only the best French wines instead of coffee or tea.

Included among Whistler's friends and the collectors of his paintings were the Leylands, prosperous Liverpool shipowners who had bought a mansion in London. An architect and interior decorator were engaged to select furnishings and artifacts for their new home. Venetian statues, mosaic floors and screens, wood paneling, tapestries, cordovan leather were gathered from every exotic and expensive corner of the world. Whistler's painting of a girl in a Japanese kimono was to be hung over the mantelpiece.

During the alteration the Leylands left London for Liverpool, and Whistler moved in and took charge. He was determined that his painting would have a proper setting. For twelve hours a day, for every day throughout the entire summer of 1876, he worked with feverish excitement. When friends came to visit, Whistler told them, "I am doing the most beautiful thing that has ever been done—the most beautiful room!"

Almost delirious with joy, he worked on into the winter, converting the entire room into a "Peacock's Paradise." Designs were painted on the invaluable cordovan leather, and he covered the walls, panels, mosaics, ceiling, and woodwork—the entire room—with peacocks painted in gold and blue harmonies.

The interior decorator, after having been locked out for months, managed at last to force his way in, only to run wildly from the house and back to his own home. There, he painted his bedroom floor blue, took to his bed, covered his head with his pillow—and a few weeks later died in an insane asylum.

"To be sure, that's the effect I have on people," Whistler said casually.

Hearing of his decorator's death, Leyland rushed back from Liverpool. His house had become a gallery, with Whistler seemingly ensconced as its director. The "Peacock's Paradise" left Leyland livid and speechless with rage. "You should be grateful," Whistler said. "I have made you famous. My work will live on when you are long forgotten." The final blow came when he handed Leyland a bill for two thousand guineas for services rendered—and with seeming reluctance settled for half.

After Leyland's death the house was sold in 1892. The American millionaire Charles L. Freer bought the room and shipped it to Detroit. It was later installed in the Freer Museum in Washington, D.C., where it can still be seen.

Mad as Whistler's escapade seemed, it was instrumental in revolutionizing interior decoration by the substitution of white walls for dark Victorian interiors, and plain walls of varied colors instead of decorated and ornamented wallpapers. A craze for Chinese porcelain and Japanese prints in the 1860s was started in England by Whistler who had introduced them from France.

A group of nine pictures exhibited at the Grosvenor Gallery in London drew the wrath of the eminent critic John Ruskin. "I have seen and heard much of Cockney impudence before now," Ruskin wrote in reviewing a "Nocturne," "but never expected a coxcomb [Whistler] to ask 200 guineas for flinging a pot of paint in the public's face."

Whistler's painting of a girl in a Japanese kimono hangs over the fire-place in the Peacock Room. FREER GALLERY OF ART, WASHINGTON, D.C.

Whistler promptly sued Ruskin for libel and the court trial became a carnival for the public who resented the artist's high-handed attitudes and challenging scorn. The trial has been called, "The most stupid, famous, ridiculous and significant case in the history of art." Whistler, mustering all his wit, brilliance, and fiery temper, declared war on a public that expected a judge and jury to decide on the merits of a painting.

Asked by Ruskin's lawyer how long it took him to complete one of his "Nocturne" paintings, Whistler replied, "One or two days."

"And that was the labor for which you asked 200 guineas?" the lawyer replied.

"No," Whistler answered. "It was for the knowledge gained through a lifetime."

Examined and questioned by the jury, Whistler snapped an

angry reply: "It is as impossible for me to explain to you the beauty of that picture as it would be for a musician to explain to you the beauty of harmony in a particular piece of music if you had no ear for music."

Artists were called in as witnesses by both sides, and the trial dissolved into a field day for conservative and academic attacks on Whistler and the entire Impressionist movement.

The judge ruled in favor of Whistler and awarded him one farthing as damages. "The case never should have been brought into court in the first place," he grumbled.

Hardly satisfied with his victory, Whistler called the trial a conspiracy. "They all hoped they could drive me out of the country or kill me," he complained. Evidently they succeeded in the first half of their wish, at least temporarily. The expenses of the trial forced him into bankruptcy. He sold his house with all its contents—all his china, prints, and several paintings—to pay off his debts and left for Venice to complete a series of etchings. His etchings had always been high in the public's esteem, and he was confident they would sell fast and enable him to bounce rapidly back from his financial embarrassment.

He returned to London in a pugnacious and hypersensitive mood, on the defensive but ready to attack. Artists, he now maintained, were superior beings, and ordinary citizens were too dull, gross, and imperceptive to understand the finer qualities of either an artist or his work. According to the critic and writer E. P. Richardson, "He transferred to England and America the war of words between the bohemian and the bourgeois then raging in Paris: a war in which insults and scorn took the place of interest and curiosity as the normal relation between the artist and his fellow man. . . . Today the artist looks on the layman as a fellow of no perception; and the most generally held layman's belief about art is that if one can understand an artist he can't be a very good one. It is a far cry from this to the concept of inevitability and universality of great art."

He had neither students nor followers. Aloof and detached from typical and common themes, he portrayed personal and imaginative qualities quite different from American art of his time or the previous centuries.

Whistler took the twenty-one-year-old Oscar Wilde under his wing as a protégé and disciple. For two years the young writer and the older artist were inseparable. When Wilde, emerging as a personality, began to steal the spotlight from his mentor, the friendship collapsed and a niggling, backbiting rivalry was born. Wilde's lecture tour in America was so successful that reporters began quoting him and ignoring Whistler, which was more than the artist could tolerate. At a lecture at the Royal Academy, he accused Wilde of stealing his opinions and criticisms. "The man is a literary thief!" he roared.

Wilde answered in an essay, ". . . he stood there, a miniature Mephistopheles, mocking the majority."

With the newspapers now looking the other way, Whistler fought back by writing and publishing his own book, *The Gentle Art of Making Enemies.*

"My bible," he called this compendium of gossip, vitriol, and sarcasm, "the story of my life." Hoping to create a hurricane, all he had bred was a squall. The critics attacked it mildly and promptly forgot it.

An egomaniac, a goad, a coxcomb, a thorn in the side of the public, a self-proclaimed superior being, he was nevertheless a great artist, and American art owes much to him. But he was an intolerable person.

When his pet poodle contracted a throat disease, he called in London's busiest and most prominent throat specialist, Sir Morell Mackenzie. With surprise, annoyance, and indignation the specialist examined the dog, prescribed treatment, pocketed a huge fee, and left.

The next day Whistler was summoned to the doctor's home. "I wanted to confer with you about painting," the doctor greeted Whistler at the front door.

"Yes?" the artist said.

"Here," the doctor said, pointing to a scratch on the door panel. "How much would you charge to paint it?"

To the very end, Whistler was a walking advertisement of himself, hoping that people who noticed him would notice his work. But he was misunderstood, and, in his day, so was his work.

In 1864, when Mary Cassatt was twenty, she announced to her stunned Victorian family that she not only had decided to become an artist but that she intended to earn money from her art.

Her father, a very proper, conservative Philadelphia banker, forbade it. Her brother, who later became president of the Pennsylvania Railroad, insisted that nice girls from leading families of Huguenot background just didn't do such shameful things. But Mary did.

She enrolled at the Pennsylvania Academy of Fine Arts. There she copied paintings, worked from casts, and shortly announced that she was leaving for Italy where art had a tradition and was closer to life. That was 1866. She spent the rest of her life in Europe.

In Italy she studied the paintings of Correggio, a sixteenth-century artist, and from his work she derived many of the influences that shaped her lifetime's work. She discovered a softness in the modeling of forms, a gentleness of expression, and, most importantly, she discovered the charm of children.

From Italy she moved to Paris, the center of the art world. There, in 1873, she saw the work that would really shape her destiny, the pastels of Degas. She drew influences from many sources, from the realistic painting of Courbet, Manet, and Pissarro, but always she returned to the work of Degas. Her admiration for the French painter was so great that, although she did not meet him for several years, her work took on a quality that was unmistakable. The first time Degas saw one of Cassatt's paintings on exhibit, he turned to a friend and said, "There is someone who feels as I do."

She found an apartment near the Louvre and painted for long, hard hours, sometimes from eight in the morning until darkness. Then during the evening she turned her attention to etching, to develop greater control and more precision of line. More and more she adopted the Parisian way of life. Her paintings were

exhibited with those of other great artists. She found life so
satisfying in the French capital that her father, mother, and sister,
despairing of her ever coming home, left her brothers in Philadelphia and moved to Paris to join her. They were so well
adjusted to her life as an artist that occasionally they contributed
to her career by serving as models.

Mary Cassatt was well-bred, social, wealthy, talented; her home
became a meeting place for the sophisticated and influential peo-
ple of Paris. Clemenceau, the great statesman, Mallarmé, the
poet, George Moore, the writer, were among her guests. Berthe
Morisot, the great-granddaughter of the eighteenth-century artist
Fragonard and a talented painter herself who later married
Manet's brother, became a close friend. Inevitably Cassatt met
Degas.

Degas was a bachelor in his forties, ten years older than Cassatt.
Surly, biting, sarcastic, the most financially successful of the Impressionists, he was always kind and generous to Cassatt. They
began working together, and sometimes she posed for him. Under
his influence she began working in pastels, gaining new and brilliant color effects. And under his influence she withdrew her
work from the salon and became a member of the Independents,
the Impressionists. Now she associated with and discussed art
with Pissarro, Monet, Manet, Renoir, Gauguin and their friends.
She showed with them at the famed Fourth Impressionist Exhibition at the Rue de L'Opéra in 1879. Critical reviews were hostile, as they were for all the Impressionists, but Cassatt was encouraged by several favorable comments and the purchase of
several of her works.

She helped ease the financial burden on many of her French
friends by encouraging wealthy American acquaintances to buy
their works. Her own paintings were sent to America for exhibition at the Society of American Artists in New York and at the
Pennsylvania Academy of Fine Arts in Philadelphia. But they
met with a disappointing lack of enthusiasm, especially in her
own home city and from members of her own family.

In 1883, the famed London-American artist, Whistler visited
Cassatt. He had been working on a portrait of her brother's wife,

and he was curious about the rich American lady painter. Evidently she was equally as curious. "He came with a cane about three and a half feet high and a glass in his eye," she wrote her brother.

"Oscar Wilde and he [Whistler] together are just about as crazy a pair of men as can be found on the face of the earth," her brother replied, filling her in with the latest of London's gossip.

She had encouraged the purchase of Impressionist paintings mainly to help support the painters. By 1886 she realized she had been doing her wealthy friends in America the greater favor— that the Impressionists were the artists of the future and that their work was a valuable investment for the purchaser and an immense cultural advantage to the nation. Serving seriously as consultant, she advised the Havemeyer family and Mrs. Potter Palmer of Chicago, wealthy ladies gathering treasures for their Victorian·palaces, to pass over the classicists and concentrate on the Impressionists. Durand Ruel, Paris' famed gallery director and collector, supported her faith in her friends and arranged to exhibit the Impressionists in New York. A large collection, including two paintings by Cassatt, were shown. While there were several favorable reviews, Impressionism was still too far ahead of the times to be appreciated, especially in Victorian America.

Along with Whistler and the other Impressionists, Cassatt came under the spell of the Japanese printmakers. Increasingly, as the years went by, her paintings took on more of the qualities of the Japanese. As the influence increased, she turned more toward the production of her own prints, working in color as well as line. Degas, her longtime friend but ever the masculine chauvinist, upon seeing one of her new color prints, exclaimed in admiration, "I do not admit it could have been done by a woman!"

Some critics found her prints more original, and therefore superior, to her paintings. The critic Adelyn D. Breeskin wrote: "In them we find her main characteristics, such as the originality of vision, the elimination of nonessentials, the arabesque quality of asymmetrical design, the strong linear pattern, the unconventional angle of perspective and well articulated rounded forms . . ." Her prints are, he went on, "her most original contribution . . . and as color prints have never been surpassed."

An exhibition of her prints brought about this comment from the Metropolitan Museum of Art: "The prints of Miss Cassatt are perhaps unique among all the prints that have ever been made in the world for a very curious and interesting reason. They represent easy, nice, clean people; pleasant women and fat babies, quietly and simply without any fuss or nonsense of cooing or other sentimentality. There is no parade of artistry or special techniques. Just as the artist was learned in the traditions of her craft, she was learned in the plain, pleasant facts of family life."

Inspired by an exhibition of Japanese prints in 1890, Cassatt began to translate more and more of her print discoveries into her painting. It was after this date that she produced some of her most luminous and mature oils and pastels. She brought to them an observant and precise draftsmanship, radiant color, and tenderness without sentimentality or overemphasis.

She had always loved children. She had used them as subjects in her prints. At the age of forty-five, perhaps in reaction to her disappointment because her friendship with Degas had never developed into marriage and motherhood, she turned to the theme of mother and child. It is this theme with which her name has always been associated. In her art she never idealized her children. Each child always maintained his own particular identity. No two were ever alike.

The Durand Ruel Gallery honored her in 1891 with her first one-man show. Her work was so well received by both press and purchasers that a second show was scheduled immediately for 1893, and that show, too, was a great success. According to one critic, "Miss Cassatt is perhaps, besides Whistler, the only artist of high talent, personable, distinguished, whom America actually possesses."

Pissarro, the old man of Impressionism, wrote, "She has a very impressive show at Durand Ruel's. She is really very able." From Pissarro that was high praise, indeed.

That same year Mrs. Potter Palmer commissioned her to paint three panels on the theme of modern woman in the fashions and attitudes of the day for the main gallery of the Women's Building

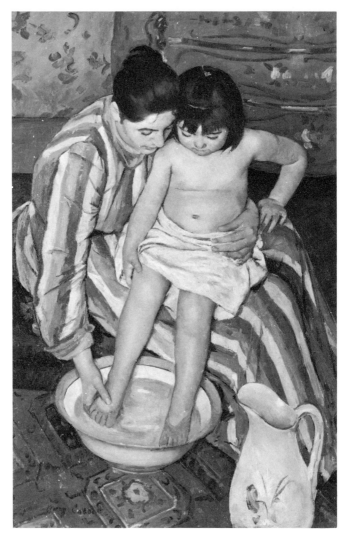

"The Bath" by Mary Cassatt. COURTESY OF THE ART INSTITUTE OF CHICAGO

of the Columbia Exposition in Chicago. This was Cassatt's first commission in America. Unfortunately the panels disappeared with the destruction of the exposition.

The Havemeyers returned to Europe seeking still more paintings. Cassatt accompanied them on a picture-buying tour of Italy and Spain, adding Veronese, El Greco, Velázquez, and Goya to their already outstanding collection of Impressionists and earlier French painters. Many of these paintings are now part of the

Havemeyer collection in the Metropolitan Museum of Art.

By the late 1890s long-deserved honors began coming her way. She rejected the Lippincott prize of the Pennsylvania Academy and the Harris prize of the Chicago Institute. "I have for too long been a member of the Independents," she said, "who formed a society in which there would be no jury, no medals, no awards."

At the turn of the century, however, she did accept the ribbon that made her a Chevalier of the Legion of Honor. "I do not need to see this ribbon," her old friend Clemenceau told her, "to know you are a great painter."

Writing of her latest work, one European critic said, "She is wholly original . . . her art expresses her nation, young, full of force. She is without prejudice, vital; there is the freshness of a new nation in her art. She expresses the character of the American people, a people awakening to all that is best in art and eager to possess in abundance."

Another said of her, "She gave this hackneyed mother and child theme a new freshness by stripping it of all artifices and literature. . . . Mary Cassatt made a very personal and important contribution to the body of Impressionist creation."

Toward the end of her life Degas, her close friend of forty years, went blind and died, and Mary Cassatt's sight began to fail as cataracts developed in her eyes. She had lived to see the triumph of the Impressionists. But she was always discouraged with the lack of full appreciation by her own family and by the Pennsylvania Academy, which, after all, represented the city of Philadelphia—her city, second in her heart only to Paris.

With her vision fast fading, she continued painting through the years of World War I. When the armistice was signed, she could barely see. A few years later America's first great lady of art was totally blind, and in 1926 she died in France.

If Mary Cassatt had never painted a picture in her life, she would still deserve to be included in the history of American art and taste because of all she did to secure paintings for this nation by acting as consultant to the great American collectors of the Victorian Era.

11

ARCHITECTS
OF THE
AMERICAN
RENAISSANCE

Not in quite the same manner that the first Puritan faced the New England wilderness with ax in hand, the Vermont-born architect Richard Morris Hunt faced 130,000 acres of Great Smoky Mountains forest and lakes near Asheville, North Carolina. In his vault was authorization from George Washington Vanderbilt, younger brother of Cornelius and William K. Vanderbilt, to spend not more than five million dollars to plan and construct a modest Victorian palace suitable for his patron.

His first step was to conduct Vanderbilt on a tour of the Continent, searching for inspiration among the châteaux along the Loire. He engaged several hundred foreign artisans for the job ahead.

Five years and $4,100,000 later, with its foundation alone covering five acres, Biltmore was completed. It opened on Christmas Eve of 1895, five months after its creator, Hunt, had died. The mansion marked the ultimate attempt to utilize the elegant designs of the past to house the American present and symbolize the most grandiose, and perhaps the final, milestone in the Victorian Era.

Biltmore, the mansion designed by Richard Morris Hunt for George Washington Vanderbilt. COURTESY OF THE BILTMORE ESTATE

A village was built nearby for workers and servants, complete with school buildings, shopping center, and hospital. A forester was hired to oversee the timberlands. Eleven million specimens grew in the arboretum of the Vanderbilt who dreamed of being America's patron of forestry and farming. Pleasure gardens were designed that rivaled those of the Rothschilds, the most conspicuously elegant family of Europe. After a visit, the secretary of agriculture reported to the President, "He [Vanderbilt] employs more men than I have in my charge."

Today Biltmore is a museum.

The architect Richard M. Hunt was born in Brattleboro, Vermont, in 1827, the younger brother of the artist William Morris Hunt. The son of a congressman, he grew up in Washington's most elegant society, went to Europe to study at Geneva and at the École des Beaux-Arts in Paris. He traveled throughout Europe, to Asia Minor and Egypt, and returned to Paris to be commissioned to design the Pavillon de la Bibliothèque. Nine years of travel, study, and work abroad provided him with more extensive and thorough training than any other American architect of his age.

Returning to America, he worked on the Capitol in Washington, married a prominent society woman, established a firm in New York City, and developed a clientele among the wealthiest and most distinguished families of the country. He enhanced Fifth Avenue with châteaux and Ocean Drive in Newport with "cottages" that were in reality tremendous year-round villas. The house built in Newport for Henry Gurdon Marquand in 1872 still stands, although it has long since been converted into apartments.

In New Haven, Yale University commissioned him to design a building to house the "Scroll and Key," one of Old Eli's undergraduate secret societies. In keeping with the mysterious rites for which the building is used, the structure itself is a mystery, with its entrance a secret known only to members of the society. A Spanish-Moorish cube of masonry, its wide bands of light stone are relieved with narrow bands of darker stone. In New York

An aerial view of The Breakers, a seventy-room mansion that resembles villas built during the Renaissance in northern Italy. COURTESY RHODE ISLAND DEVELOPMENT COUNCIL

Hunt designed the colossal pedestal for the Statue of Liberty, a great, lofty mass that easily supports the huge figure created by the French sculptor Auguste Bartholdi and engineered by Gustave Eiffel. The pedestal is a masterwork of proportion and ornament, in perfect scale with the huge statue in its harbor setting.

Despite his successes and clientele, Hunt remained an indefatigable worker. He advised his employees, "You've got to work days, and you've got to work nights. When you wake up during the night, you've got to think about the project!" Seeing one of his associates on the dance floor one night, he stormed at him, "What are you doing here! You should be at home, sketching!"

As Hunt grew older, his work improved. More and more he drew his inspiration from the French architects of the sixteenth century, particularly from Renaissance châteaux along the Loire that he had seen and admired during his years in France. After the age of fifty, during the last fifteen years of his life, he scored his most brilliant successes.

In 1888 he built Ochre Court for Ogden Goelet, on a choice lot on Newport's cliffs. The main hall in this Gothic château rose several stories high with a gilded, encrusted, and painted ceiling reminiscent of the Paris Opéra. Today Ochre Court houses a Roman Catholic school for girls.

For Cornelius Vanderbilt he remodeled The Breakers in Newport into three million dollars' worth of gigantic and chilly Italian villa in the manner of sixteenth-century Genoa, with a double staircase wide enough to service a railway station. For. W. K. Vanderbilt he planned and constructed a sixteenth-century French-style château with rounded turrets, mansard roofs, and Renaissance details that stretched along New York City's Fifth Avenue from Fifty-first Street to Fifty-second. A critic wrote of this building, "Like a more perfect Pompeii, the work will be a vision and an image of a typical American residence, seized at the moment when the nation begins to have a taste of its own."

Like most other Victorian excesses, this vision, too, was torn

An interior view of The Breakers showing the magnificent Great Hall.
COURTESY OF THE PRESERVATION SOCIETY OF NEWPORT COUNTY, NEWPORT, RHODE ISLAND

down. It lasted until 1926 when it was wrecked to make way for New York's burgeoning skyscrapers.

As trusts replaced individual businesses, so did professional architects and architectural firms replace the nameless artisan and the independent builder.

The American Institute of Architects was founded in 1857. Massachusetts Institute of Technology founded its architectural school in 1866. The first architectural journal appeared in Philadelphia in 1868. The age of specialization had begun.

Before 1860, American architecture followed certain rigid patterns. Neither materials nor structural theories varied in any great degree from those of the ancient Greeks and Romans. Building types were few and simple, easily constructed and erected. There was no sharp difference, except in size, between the homes for the upper and lower classes of society. A large, powerful wealthy class had not yet emerged; taste was democratic and diffused.

By the end of the nineteenth century, low-cost, mass-produced steel began to replace iron which had gradually replaced wood for structural supports. Portland cement manufacture, begun in 1870 at Coplay, Pennsylvania, stimulated construction with brick, stone, and masonry. With the industrialization of glass manufacturing, huge plate glass windows began to appear on Victorian houses, bringing light to the previously dark interiors. Wood, abundant and cheap, was still America's favorite building material . . . and power-driven jigsaws and lathes cut, turned, and twisted it into the gingerbread motifs so popular during the Victorian Age.

Architecture began to take on new forms. The telephone and pneumatic tube made possible the huge expansion of stores. Elevators made upper floors as accessible as lower ones. With telephones and loudspeakers, five hundred workmen could be directed as easily as one, and factories were enlarged. Motors, wires, control of electrical current made it possible for one man to operate machines that had formerly required the labor of many. New buildings were needed to serve new purposes, and new systems were developed to make them functional and livable.

By the end of the nineteenth century, many houses had central heat, indoor baths, and plumbing and electric lights. Cities were crowded with the influx of people needed to run the burgeoning factories. The speculator, the builder, and the engineer, rather than the architect, planned the tenements that housed the masses of immigrants, workers, laborers. The poor and the downtrodden huddled in dark and dingy rooms in overcrowded, dismal cities, while the newly rich industrialists built large, spacious, and richly ornamented homes. In town and country their mansions combined and reflected all the forms, motifs, and tastes of Europe that their architects could provide.

The work of Henry Hobson Richardson dominated the architectural trends of the 1880s. Charming, gay, and sophisticated, dressed in the latest of Victorian style by Poole of London, tailors to Britain's nobility, Richardson was the perfect image of an architect for a millionaire patronage.

He was the great-grandson of Joseph Priestley, the discoverer of oxygen who had fled to America when a British mob, outraged by his sympathies for the French Revolution, burned his house to the ground. Born on a Louisiana plantation, he matriculated at Harvard after having been rejected by West Point because of a speech defect.

After graduation he traveled to England, Scotland, and Wales and then studied architecture at the École des Beaux-Arts in Paris. When the Civil War cut him off from his allowances from home, he went to work for Théodore Labrouste, one of the leading designers of France. He remained abroad for five years, and his fiancée, growing understandably impatient, wrote, "How long will you have to remain before returning to America?"

"It depends on various things," he answered. "And you would prefer to have me remain a few months longer in Europe than to return to America a second rate architect. Our poor country is over-run with them now—I will never practice until I feel that I can at least do my art justice."

In 1865, at the age of twenty-seven, he felt he was ready. He returned to the United States, settled in Boston, and began his

career designing homes for the families of his friends. Fame arrived suddenly seven years later, when he won a competition for
the design of Boston's Trinity Church. With elements and motifs
freely drawn from the French Romanesque style of the twelfth
century, it won the praise of numerous influential people. When
this massive, dramatic masonry structure, elaborated with turrets
and pinnacles that culminated in an enormous central tower, was
completed in 1877, Richardson was swamped with commissions
for buildings and churches.

He was commissioned by the family of Oakes Ames of North
Easton, Massachusetts, to design a family memorial. Congressman Oliver Ames had founded a shovel works which was the
source of the family's wealth. By the time of his death it was
worth two hundred thousand dollars. His brother, Oakes, and
Oliver, Jr., took over, increasing their inheritance to four million
dollars by the outbreak of the Civil War—and then catapulted
this fortune to astronomical heights through investment in the
Union Pacific Railroad.

Richardson's monument designed in their memory near Lar-
amie, Wyoming, was a pyramid of solid ashlar stone that rivaled
the tombs of the ancient pharaohs of Egypt. Richardson, who had
once stated, "What I want most to design is a grain elevator and
the interior of a Mississippi steamboat," turned to the design of
railroads. In North Easton, the home of the Ameses, he built the
station, as well as the town hall, in honor of Oliver, Jr., a library
in honor of Oakes, and a gate lodge and gardener's cottage for
the son of Oliver, Jr. His railway stations in Boston and in Albany
at Chestnut Hill, and later at New London, marked the beginning of daily commuting to the cities for business.

In Chicago, Richardson built a huge warehouse for Marshall
Field. The building was the greatest of all of Richardson's designs
for the business world. Created during the year that marked the
birth of the skyscraper, it had a strong influence on Chicago's
growing school of architecture. Louis Sullivan, the leader of that
school, was so impressed that he called the massive, dignified,
yet simple structure an oasis in a desert of incredibly bad taste.
"Four square and brown it stands," he wrote, "a monument to

The warehouse designed by Henry Hobson Richardson for Marshall Field was a massive granite building resembling a Florentine palace.
COURTESY OF MARSHALL FIELD & COMPANY

trade, to organized commercial spirit, to the power and progress of the age, to the strength and resource of individuality of character: spiritually it stands as the index of a mind, large enough, courageous enough to cope with these things, master them, absorb them, and give them forth again, impressed with the stamp of a large and forceful personality."

A gigantic seven-story block of granite arranged around a central court, the warehouse resembled the palace of the Medicis and other merchant princes of fifteenth-century Florence. Cubelike, solid, formidable, its horizontal levels are marked by round arched windows, a distinctive roof line, and variations in size of bays and window openings. Unique was the directness with which the exterior design stated the nature and purpose of the building and its interior function and structure. It was torn down in 1930.

Richardson fabricated great civic monuments in a similar manner, massive and compelling—the Albany City Hall in 1882 and the Pittsburgh courthouse and prison, which he did not live long enough to see completed. His Crane Memorial Library at Quincy, Massachusetts, still stands as one of his most famed designs for smaller buildings. The library reveals Richardson's mastery with French Romanesque style, granite construction, and the arrangement of huge masses of stone without compromise.

His most distinguished designs for mansions were at Newport, summer capital of the Eastern millionaires. Now Newport is famed as the site of the summer folk and jazz festivals, a magnet for all Americans, young and old, rich and poor alike. The William Watts Sherman house, completed in 1876, still stands as a Baptist old people's home. Its bold geometric shapes, its rich textures of stone, brick, wood, plaster, and shingle set it clearly apart from Newport's other Victorian overstatements. Scholars believe its half-timbered construction was influenced by the English homes built by Norman Shaw as a reaction against Victorian elegance—and in admiration of Elizabethan times. Part of a merry-go-round of improvement and improvisation, Richardson borrowed from Shaw who owed much to seventeenth-century American homes, which in turn had been modified by American architects of the seventeenth century from original Elizabethan homes found in the builders' guides that colonists had brought with them from England.

The granite walls of the first story of this vast and majestic structure are topped by thick, brown timbers—with the spaces between filled with pink stucco—and several varisized brick chimneys. Enormous landscaped grounds surround the building and add to the stateliness of the mansion. This is an estate of proportions seldom seen in America and the image of an age that has long since passed into history.

Richardson suffered from a disease that gave him the waistline of an elephant. He drank heavily but jovially and was capable of putting away a magnum of champagne and several pounds of cheese—both of which were prohibited by his doctor—at one sitting. He died in 1886 at the age of forty-seven, as grandiose a figure as the era he embellished.

While Richardson looked to the past to solve the problems of the future, Charles Follen McKim and Stanford White, who had trained in Richardson's offices and later joined with William Rutherford Mead to found the firm of McKim, Mead, and White, used the architecture of history only to speak the language of the past. But they spoke it with an eloquence that helped to give shape and character to the age.

Each member of the firm had been superbly trained in his profession. McKim had studied at Harvard and at the École des Beaux-Arts. Mead was an Amherst graduate who had worked in an architect's office and had traveled throughout Italy studying the great monuments of the past. The deep impression made by the Italian Renaissance on Mead left a distinctive stamp on the firm's work. Stanford White had been trained as a draftsman in the studio of Richardson. Immensely talented, White was a skilled designer of buildings and jewelry, the creator of graceful covers for *The Century* and *Cosmopolitan* magazines, and a fine painter. In 1879, when McKim was thirty-two, Mead thirty-three, and White twenty-six, they set up their firm in New York.

No other American architects were so deeply admired or so vehemently damned as these three men.

The young White was a spectacular character. With flaming red hair and moustache, he was the city's best dressed and best known man-about-town. He continually attracted attention and reveled in every inch of newspaper space devoted to his escapades and activities. He would arrive at the opera every night, conspicuous by his lateness, confident that every eye was on him in his center seat in the auditorium and, again, as he left only one hour later. To him, the chorus of whispers—"There's Stanford White"—was the sweetest music the opera had to offer.

Mead, a levelheaded Vermonter, was the stabilizing force of the partnership and the realistic guide of the firm's business practices. "It takes all my time," he said, "to keep my partners from making damn fools of themselves." He outlived White by twenty-two years and McKim by nineteen and kept the partnership name active until his death in 1928 on the eve of the stock market crash that brought on the great depression and finally wiped out the last vestiges of the Age of the Robber Barons.

McKim, Mead, and White dominated New York City. They set the taste and created the fashions and forms that others were glad to follow. They worked their will on the city and shaped it into the image it still retains. Indeed, they were the perfect reflection of New York in the Gay Nineties.

White drew the plans for a French Gothic castle for Mrs. W.

K. Vanderbilt to harmonize with her mother-in-law's castle next door that had been built by Hunt. But Gothic was not the firm's forte. While McKim and White were equally versed and adept in designs of all periods, Mead preferred Italian Renaissance; and what Mead wanted, Mead got.

An outstanding example of Stanford White's work in the Italian Renaissance idiom still stands on Madison Avenue in New York, used now by the Archdiocese of the Roman Catholic Church. Built in 1885 as a complex of five town houses for the railroad promoter Henry Villard and four of his friends, the structure recalls the sixteenth-century Cancelleria Palace in Rome.

They built a fantastic turreted, tower, romantic stone and shingled house on the shores of Long Island Sound in Mamaroneck, New York, for Charles J. Osborne, Jay Gould's banker; and a sheer, ground-hugging, modern-looking, horizontal triangle for G. W. Low, a nephew of a clipper ship operator, in Bristol, Rhode Island; and a Newport mansion of shingle and frame with a delicate, bamboo-supported porch that ran the entire length of the house for Isaac Bell, a cotton broker. They built the Boston Public Library in 1887 and William C. Whitney's New York mansion.

Henry Adams wrote of the millionaire Whitney: "He had thrown away the usual objects of political ambition like the ashes of a smoked cigarette . . . until New York no longer knew what most to envy, his horses or his houses." If they chose the latter, it could have been because they were designed by the firm and their interiors were planned and decorated by White.

Louis Sherry, the most gifted caterer of the age, turned to White and his partners for his elegant hotel and restaurant on Forty-fourth Street and Fifth Avenue. The building and its lavish salons were never outshone, not even by the dress, jewels, and coiffures of the patrons, some of the most elegant ladies and gentlemen of the world. To complement the designs of the Tiffany jewels, the firm built the Tiffany House, a jewel of architecture on upper Madison Avenue. The old Madison Square Garden was their design as well as the Madison Square Presbyterian Church and the Herald Tribune Building. Off their drafting boards came the Century Club, the Metropolitan Club, the University Club, the

Harvard Club, and the J. P. Morgan library. The important people of the world passed through portals they had designed and lunched in the elegant dining rooms they had decorated.

In the manner of the great Roman temples of Caracalla, they built the Pennsylvania Railroad Station, and their classic inspiration is evident in the halls and campus of Columbia University.

The stucco and shingled walls, the classic forms of Wheatly Hills on Long Island recall early Philadelphia Georgian mansions. This great country house, planned for Edwin D. Morgan, grandson of the banker, was huge, rambling, and U-shaped with secluded courtyard, a family wing on one side, and a servants' quarter on the other. The structure covered acres of green land in Roslyn. Today it is surrounded by upper middle-class housing developments, lost in the maze of New York's suburbia.

When Mrs. Clarence Mackey, daughter-in-law of the principal stockholder in the Comstock lode, wanted a château on a hill in Roslyn, second only to the Vanderbilt's Biltmore, she called on Stanford White. The design, based on the Maison Lafitte outside of Paris, with influences both Italian and French in the Louis XV manner, was easy for the talented White to deliver. But he had a more time-consuming problem with the furnishings. In the cellar he installed a wine rack large enough for 21,900 bottles. So, naturally, it was the duty of the consummate Victorian Age architect to fill that rack. Off he went to explore the cellars and salons of Europe—to Munich, Burgos, Dresden, Berlin, Vienna, Palermo, Florence, Malta, Barcelona, Seville, Cordova, Madrid, Oporto, Lisbon, Brussels, Amsterdam, London, Bordeaux, Reims, Marseilles, and Paris—seeking chairs, tapestries, and rugs; beds, tables, and decorations—and the best of all the vintage wines the Old World could offer.

The Pennsylvania Station is gone, and so is Sherry's. Wheatley Hills is altered beyond recognition. Madison Square Garden, the Herald Tribune Building—newspaper and all—are gone. The country estates are schools and homes for the aged, retreats for union organizations, study centers for colleges.

As the population of America burgeoned, because of the never-ending stream of immigration during the seventies, eighties, and nineties, cities doubled and tripled in size. Vast new territories were settled; factories, schools, and homes sprang up across the land. As in the Puritan and early pioneering days, a huge part of this building was done without architect, engineer, or professional advice of any kind. There were still builders' guides and handbooks for carpenters, and new Americans—as self-reliant as the originals had been—built, improvised, planned, tinkered, invented, and changed. Yankees they weren't. But they adopted the Yankee tradition and found practical answers when the going got rough.

The best and most frequent answer for the practical carpenter was the "balloon house," invented in Chicago in 1833, and so called because traditional builders had sneered that they would blow away like balloons in a high wind. Some did. But most hung together and were easily put in place again. Thousands remained where they were built, especially after a technique was developed for bolting them to the foundation, and they contributed more to the rapid expansion of America than any other single building factor.

The balloon house was made possible by the technological improvements of the age. It was technology that caused most of the changes in America's methods and types of home building. The settlers of the seventeenth century had brought with them the concept of skeletal structure that can still be seen in old wood frame houses and barns. Parts were all handworked, crude, and inexact. Walling merely filled spaces between the beams but seldom supported the ceilings or roof, strengthened the structure, or protected the skeleton from the climate, especially in the extremes of New England. Thus, deterioration was usually rapid.

Modifications occurred as changes in technology were made. Shingles and shakes could be made by hand, but clapboards and flooring required sawing, and sawing was a tedious and laborious job. Structural timbers were more exact, and their production could be speeded up by sawing. Sawmills had no tradition in England. In fact, they had even been forbidden. But in the colonies building had to move at a faster pace than in the mother country, so the first water-powered sawmills appeared in 1633 at Piscataqua

Falls on the line that separated the New Hampshire colony from the Maine wilderness.

By the eighteenth century a gigantic lumber industry had emerged, spurred on by the steam-powered sawmill. But house-building, with pegs and mortises and bolts at the corner, and the exorbitant cost of handmade nails, still progressed at a comparative crawl. Then in the 1830s, with the invention of wire-cut nails, handmade parts were abandoned, and the balloon house came into being. The house itself was lightened and labor on the building site was drastically reduced, and the housing sprint was on.

Most balloon frames followed the design of the still popular Cape Cod Cottage. The basic parts, mostly two-by-four studs and plates, cut to proper length on the site by a handsaw, ran the entire height of the building and were nailed together, creating the light and sturdy frame that was later braced and crossbraced and sheathed for protection inside and out. By 1840, in the Midwest, typical frame houses were built completely of elements milled and prepared away from the actual site of the building. With little variation and some added features this technique has become standard for the building of houses today.

Even most modern so-called brick and stone houses, instead of being built of solid material, are merely a masonry façade on top of wooden balloon framing. "If it had not been for knowledge of the balloon house," one historian wrote, "Chicago and San Francisco could never have risen as they did, from little villages to great cities in a single year."

Certainly anyone who has seen sprawling Levittown and other suburban single-home communities rise by the thousands in ever-expanding circles on the periphery of the nation's cities, or any-one who has ever seen a carpenter or nonspecialist remodel a room, is familiar with balloon framing and the balloon house.

It stands by the multimillions, mostly white, and made of wood. It has been modified with expansion attics, playrooms, dormers and carports, in variations from the conformity of the com-munities and shaped to the individual use, need, and purpose of the owner. And, mostly, it sits back a proper and practical dis-tance on a bright green lawn. It is the house of America today.

BIBLIOGRAPHY

Andrews, Wayne. *Architecture, Ambition and Americans.* New York: Harper and Brothers, 1955.

Eliot, Alexander. *Three Hundred Years of American Painting.* New York: Time, Inc., 1957.

Fitch, James M. *American Building.* Boston: Houghton Mifflin Company, 1966.

Flexner, James T. *That Wilder Image.* Boston: Little, Brown, 1962.

Goodrich, Lloyd. *Winslow Homer.* New York: The Macmillan Company, 1945.

Gowans, Alan. *Images of American Living.* New York: J. B. Lippincott, 1964.

Hamlin, Talbot. *Greek Revival Architecture in America.* New York: Oxford University Press, 1944.

Larkin, Oliver W. *Art and Life in America.* New York: Holt, Rinehart and Winston, 1960.

McCracken, H. *George Catlin and the Old Frontier.* New York: Dial Press, 1959.

Mendelowitz, Daniel M. *A History of American Art.* New York: Holt, Rinehart and Winston, 1960.

Pearson, Hesketh. *The Man Whistler.* New York: Harper and Brothers, 1952.

Richardson, E. P. *Painting in America.* New York: Thomas Y. Crowell, 1956.

Sweet, Frederick. *Miss Mary Cassatt.* Norman, Oklahoma: University of Oklahoma Press, 1966.

INDEX

709.73
MYR

5067

Myron, Robert.

Art in America from colonial
days through the nineteenth
century.